Barnes & Noble Critical Studies

General Editor: Anne Smith

The Art of Brendan Behan

THE ART OF
BRENDAN BEHAN

edited by

E. H. Mikhail

BOOKS
10 East 53d St., New York 10022
(a division of Harper & Row Publishers, Inc.)

Barnes & Noble Books
Harper & Row, Publishers, Inc.
10 East 53rd Street
New York

ISBN 0–06–494825–0
LC No. 79–50930

First published in the U.S.A. 1979
© 1979 Vision Press

Printed and bound in Great Britain
MCMLXXIX

Table of Contents

Acknowledgements

The editor and publishers wish to thank the following who have kindly given permission for the use of copyright material:

The *Daily Telegraph* for the article: "Brendan Behan: 'Uproarious Tragedy' " by Alan Brien.

The *New Statesman* for the articles: "O'Casey Goes to Jail" by Maurice Richardson; and "Early and Late" by Desmond MacNamara.

A. D. Peters & Co. Ltd. for the article: "Behan: A Giant of a Man, Yet Gentle" by Kenneth Allsop in the *Daily Mail*.

The Thomas More Association for the article "The Bloodshot World of Brendan Behan" in *The Critic*.

Modern Drama for the article "*An Giall* and *The Hostage* Compared" by Richard Wall.

The Tablet for the article "Death's Jest Book" by Alex Matheson Cain.

Robert Brustein for his article "Libido at Large" in *The New Republic*.

The *Illustrated London News* for the article "Go-As-You Please" by J. C. Trewin.

The American Theatre Association for the article "The Heroic Dimension in Brendan Behan's *The Hostage*" by Gordon M. Wickstrom.

The *Irish Press* for the article "Brendan Behan" by Francis MacManus.

The *Saturday Review* for the following articles: "The Quare World of Brendan Behan" by Henry Hewes; "Streets Broad and Narrow" by Michael Campbell; and "The Side Streets of Dublin" by A. M. Sullivan.

ACKNOWLEDGEMENTS

The *Evening Herald* for the article "Behan's Play with Hardly a Leg to Stand on" by John Finegan.

The *Observer* for the articles: "The End of the Noose" and "New Amalgam" by Kenneth Tynan; "The Two Faces of Ireland" by Louis MacNeice; "The Quare Fellow" by Irving Wardle; "Behan on Tape" by Maurice Richardson; and "A Behan Celebration" by Robert Brustein.

The *Chicago Tribune* for the articles: *"The Scarperer"* by Richard Sullivan; " 'To Show That Still She Lives' " by Frank O'Connor; and "A Raucous, Witty Tour of Ireland" by Richard Ellmann. Reprinted, courtesy of the *Chicago Tribune*.

The *Times Literary Supplement* for the articles: "Pen and Gab"; "Journalism"; "Hostage in New York"; and "Death and the Irish".

The *London Magazine* for the article "The Writings of Brendan Behan" by Colin MacInnes.

World Literature Today for the article "Brendan Behan" by Stanley Weintraub.

Ariel: A Review of International English Literature for the article "Borstal Boy: A Portrait of the Artist as a Young Prisoner" by Colbert Kearney.

Tribune for the article "Waiting for the Hangman" by Richard Findlater.

Studies for the article *"The Hostage"* by Thomas Kilroy. The Morris Library, Southern Illinois University at Carbondale, for the article "Borstal Revisited" by Corey Phelps in *I Carb S*.

The editor has made every effort to trace the copyright holders, but if he has inadvertently overlooked any, he will be pleased to make the necessary arrangements at the first opportunity.

Biographical Table

1923 Feb. 9	Brendan Behan born in Dublin, the first child of Stephen and Kathleen (Kearney) Behan. Mrs. Behan had been married before to Jack Furlong, who left her a young widow with two sons, Rory and Sean, the latter a favourite of Brendan.
1928–34	Attends School of the French Sisters of Charity of St. Vincent de Paul, North William Street, Dublin.
1931	Joins Fianna Eireann [the Republican scout organisation founded by Countess Markievicz].
1934–37	Attends Irish Christian Brothers' School at St. Canice's, North Circular Road, Dublin.
1937	Attends Bolton Street Technical School to learn the trade of house-painting.
	Dublin Corporation relocates the Behans in a housing estate in Crumlin.
	Joins the Irish Republican Army (I.R.A.), transferring from Fianna Eireann.
1939 Nov.	Arrested in Liverpool for illegal I.R.A. activity and held in Walton Jail.
1940 Feb.	Tried and sentenced to three years' Borstal (i.e. reform) treatment in Hollesley Bay Borstal Institution, Suffolk, England.
1941 Nov.	Released and deported to Ireland under an Expulsion Order.
1942 Apr.	Shooting incident at Glasnevin Cemetery, Dublin, on the day of the annual Easter Sunday commemoration of the Rising of 1916; sentenced to fourteen years for shooting at a policeman; begins sentence in Mountjoy Prison, Dublin.
June	"I Become a Borstal Boy", his first story published in *The Bell*.
1943 July	Transferred to Arbour Hill Military Prison.
1944 June	Transferred to Curragh Military Camp.

11

1946 Nov.		Released from prison in the General Amnesty.
1946–51		House-painter, seaman and smuggler.
1947 Jan.		Goes to the Blasket Islands, County Kerry.
	Mar.	Arrested in Manchester for attempting to free an I.R.A. prisoner from an English Jail.
	July	Released from Strangeways Jail.
1948 May		Sentenced to one month with hard labour in Mountjoy Prison for assaulting a policeman.
	Aug.	Goes to live in Paris.
1951–56		Free-lance journalist.
1952 Oct.		Arrested at Newhaven for breaking deportation order.
	Nov.	Released from Lewes Prison, Sussex; visits Samuel Beckett in Paris.
1953 Oct.–Nov.		*The Scarperer*, by "Emmet Street", published serially in *The Irish Times*.
1954 Apr.		Begins weekly column in *The Irish Press*.
	Nov.	*The Quare Fellow*, directed by Alan Simpson, opens at the Pike Theatre, Dublin.
1955 Feb.		Marries Beatrice ffrench-Salkeld, daughter of the Irish artist Cecil Salkeld, at the Sacred Heart Church, Donnybrook.
1956 May		*The Quare Fellow*, directed by Joan Littlewood, opens at the Theatre Royal, Stratford, East London.
	Sept.–Oct.	*Borstal Boy* published serially in the Irish edition of the *Sunday Dispatch*.
	Nov.	*The Quare Fellow* published.
1957 Jan.		Draft of *Borstal Boy* accepted for publication by Hutchinson.
	Mar.	Begins *An Giall* (*The Hostage*) in Irish.
1958 Jan.		Goes to Ibiza, Spain.
	Apr.	Goes to Paris to discuss the production of *The Quare Fellow*.
	June	*An Giall* opens at Damer Hall, Dublin.
	Aug.	Goes to Sweden. Starts translation of *An Giall*.
	Oct.	*The Hostage*, directed by Joan Littlewood, opens at the Theatre Royal, Stratford, East London. *Borstal Boy* published.
	Nov.	*The Quare Fellow*, directed by Jose Quintero, opens off-Broadway, New York.
	Dec.	*The Hostage* published.
1959 Mar.		Goes to Berlin for the opening of *The Quare Fellow*.

12

	Apr.	Goes to Paris. *The Hostage* selected to represent Great Britain at the Théâtre des Nations Festival.
	July	*The Hostage* moves to Wyndham's Theatre in the West End of London.
		First serious breakdown.
1960	Jan.	Tapes *Brendan Behan's Island* in Dublin.
	Mar.	Begins *Richard's Cork Leg*.
		Goes to London. Second breakdown.
	Sept.	Goes to New York for the opening of *The Hostage* at the Cort Theatre.
	Dec.	Returns to Dublin.
1961	Jan.	Translates *Richard's Cork Leg* into Irish.
		Failure of *A Fine Day in the Graveyard*.
	Mar.	Travels 11,000 miles across the United States and Canada.
		Two periods in hospital.
	July	Returns to Dublin.
	Sept.–Oct.	"The Big House" published in *Evergreen Review*.
	Oct.	Film version of *The Quare Fellow* opens in London.
1962	Feb.	Returns to New York for the off-Broadway production of *The Hostage*.
	Mar.	Returns to Dublin.
	July	*The Hostage* selected in France as the best play of the season.
	Sept.	Goes to London. Enters home for alcoholics.
	Oct.	*Brendan Behan's Island* published.
	Nov.	Goes to France to recuperate.
		Returns to Dublin after failure of cure.
1963	Feb.	Final trip to America.
	Apr.	Tapes *Confessions of an Irish Rebel* in New York.
	July	Returns to Dublin and to hospital.
	Sept.	*Hold Your Hour and Have Another* published.
	Nov.	Tapes *Brendan Behan's New York* in Dublin.
		Blanaid Behan born.
	Dec.	Enters hospital.
1964	Jan.	In and out of hospital.
	Mar. 20	Dies in Meath Hospital, Dublin.
	June	*The Scarperer* published.
	Sept.	*Brendan Behan's New York* published.
1965	Sept.	*Confessions of an Irish Rebel* published.
1967		"Moving Out" and "A Garden Party", ed. Robert Hogan, published.

13

| 1972 Mar. | *Richard's Cork Leg*, directed by Alan Simpson, opens at the Abbey Theatre, Dublin. |
| 1973 | *Richard's Cork Leg* published. |

Preface

In 1968, Terence de Vere White predicted in his book *Ireland* that Brendan Behan's "literary reputation is unlikely to grow with the passage of time". Today, only ten years after this verdict was made, Behan's literary reputation has not only grown, but is still steadily growing and confirms an assumption of increasing interest in his work. One collection of reminiscences of the writer has already appeared, and another is being prepared. Biographies of him have been written by Ulick O'Connor and by members of the Behan family—Beatrice Behan, Brian Behan, Dominic Behan, and Seamus de Burca. He is still highly thought of in Dublin, and the play about him based on *Borstal Boy* was a hit of the 1967 Dublin Theatre Festival and of the 1970 theatrical season in New York. Several studies on Behan as a writer have been made. A full-length bibliography of criticism on him, comprising some 2,000 entries, will soon go to the press. The letters of Brendan Behan, though not voluminous, are being edited. At least twenty known dissertations, wholly or partially devoted to Behan, have so far been submitted to Irish, American, French, German, Swiss, Italian, and Polish universities. Another evidence of the extent of scholarly interest in his work is the publication this year (1978) of *Brendan Behan: The Complete Plays*. Furthermore, both *The Quare Fellow* and *The Hostage* have consistently been revived in various parts of the world since they were first produced in Dublin some twenty-five years ago. There is every indication, therefore, that Behan is the most important postwar Irish writer.

It is unfortunate that the legend that made Brendan Behan concentrates in the main more on his drinking attributes than on his work. A similar fate was suffered by Oscar Wilde, the critical evaluations of whose achievement vitiated themselves in accepting biased popular judgments of the writer's personality, which per-

15

vaded all he wrote. Like Wilde, Behan was an extraordinary figure both as a writer and as a man, and in order to picture him fairly, if not definitely, it is necessary to merge the two aspects of him. Both Behan and Wilde were too busy living to write, and both died suffering the agony of not being able to write any more. It is our misfortune that the full span of their respective careers bridged only a few years.

Behan's limited output, however, deserves more attention than has hitherto been accorded to it. The present anthology of articles and reviews contains material not otherwise accessible in book form. Although the stress is on Behan the writer rather than on Behan the man, some tributes to him by important contemporary writers have necessarily been included in the first section of the book in the hope that they will help the reader fully understand his writings. Since these tributes were written almost at the same time, they have been arranged according to the alphabetical order of the writers' names. The rest of the anthology has been arranged chronologically. Unless otherwise indicated, all annotations are the editor's. In the case of the reviews of the plays, a footnote has been supplied to indicate which production is being reviewed, or whether the review deals with the play production or with the published script. A biographical table has been provided at the beginning of the book for the convenient reference of the reader. Every attempt has been made by the editor to strike a balance between Irish, English, and American coverage.

E.H.M.

PART ONE

Brendan Behan the Man

1

Behan: A Giant of a Man, Yet Gentle

by KENNETH ALLSOP*

Brendan Behan's rogue elephantine talent drowned in a whiskey glass. He was an alcoholic, a big man helpless as a baby in need of its feeding bottle, who pretended to be a jolly, convivial gargler.

He always had to push the boat out to avert being stranded alone on the bleak island of his own memories and fears.

I knew Brendan well, and had paddled along behind him in the spray of his drinking bouts in London, Dublin—where he died last night—New York and sundry scatterings of pubs elsewhere.

Now, more than sadness I feel anger that he is dead—anger that the creative bounty that was rich as yolk within his huge humpty-dumpty frame was so systematically addled in booze.

But, really, it's pointless to rue all the surge of unwritten books and plays that were there where *The Quare Fellow*, *The Hostage*, and *Borstal Boy* came from. For like Dylan Thomas, who also committed suicide by drink, he was the man he was and had to do what he did.

There were two reasons why he was compelled to drown his troubled heart. He was Irish as one of his own gamey stage characters, and success and celebrity forced him to stay permanently in the glad rags of the roaring boy, the terror of pale suburbanites, the toss-pot who always tossed his pot farther than anyone else.

But behind the clown's mask—if Dylan had, in Dame Edith Sitwell's words, the "face of a fallen angel", Brendan's, with that

* The *Daily Mail* (London), (21 March 1964), p. 7.

delicate broken nose and tangled curls, was that of a ruined Caesar—was the unbearable knowledge of what he had done.

Of course he had been an I.R.A. gunman. But it was not until I was with him in New York last spring that I learned the true source of Brendan's anguish. In 1942 he came to Britain with bombs in his suitcase to strike a militant blow for the freedom cause he then passionately believed in.

The terrorist squad he was working with dropped a bomb into a pillar-box in Liverpool and it exploded and killed a young woman and her baby who were passing.

It was not only something he could never forget, but something he could never bring himself to remember if there was drink there to swill it over.

He said to me recently, when describing how he had once fired a pistol at a policeman in a 1942 Dublin battle: "Only a lunatic boasts of taking a human life. Essentially I'm a very gentle and amiable person."[1]

But behind the roistering boisterousness and the bellowed anecdotes, songs and aphorisms was a man with an appetite for living greater than his thirst for drink.

The only people he hated were those wet blankets who try to quell and diminish the blaze of life. He believed ferociously in kindliness, and he would punch anyone on the nose who advocated violence.

He was, indeed, a gentle and amiable man. More than the loss of the books he never wrote, I shall feel that henceforth there will always be an empty chair at the feast.

NOTES

Kenneth Allsop, English writer and broadcaster. His other writings on Behan include "His New Play Is Loaded," *The Irish Digest* (Dublin), LIX (March 1957), 31–32 [Interview]; and "Beneath the Froth," *The New York Times Book Review*, (12 May 1968), p. 10 [Recollections].

1   "I reflected on the sadness of Irishmen fighting Irishmen or indeed, I'm ashamed even now to say, of men fighting men or men fighting women or women fighting women anywhere, because at heart I'm a pacifist." — *Brendan Behan, Confessions of an Irish Rebel* (London: Hutchinson, 1965), p. 51.

2

Brendan Behan:
"Uproarious Tragedy"

by ALAN BRIEN*

Brendan Behan first came to ad-mass fame as the "Television Irishman" when he sang his songs, cursed his curses and flapped his arms before the uneasy eye of the B.B.C. camera.

He leaped into pop fame like an egg into a fan. He was a one-man Beatle quartet—an omelette served up from a mixed bowl of Gilbert Harding, Dylan Thomas and Michael Collins.

Theatre critics and discerning play-goers had for some time known a different—if sometimes disturbingly similar—figure, the author of *The Quare Fellow* and *The Hostage*. He was one of the first dramatists on the British stage to open the steps leading into an underworld where a new and alarming repertoire of characters introduced themselves.

He forced us to watch men at the end of their tether, men facing death and humiliation and loneliness with humour and spirit. Behan cared about men at work—and his definition of work included crime, politics, drinking and unemployment.

The Hostage was, in his phrase, "an uproarious tragedy". In this he came nearer to his public image when he created that roaring outing of a broth of a bhoy, that wild Synge-song in an Irish stew, which carried audiences away on a frothing wave of talk and song.

Sometimes, in private and with his friends, he still wore the glowing mask of Battling Brendan. I remember a Dublin night when he insisted upon giving me the pleasure of his voice raised in rebel ballads. Knowing the English reluctance to listen to the voice of ancient independence, he took the precaution of linking his little

* The *Sunday Telegraph* (London), (22 March 1964), p. 19.

21

finger through the top button of my waistcoat. The concert began, and went on and on and on. After half an hour I unslipped my waistcoat and went to the kitchen for a drink. Two hours later, I returned to find Brendan, eyes closed, still crooning into my watch pocket.

There was also Brendan the defier of illness and denier of mortality, who exposed his body and brain to punishment beyond the call of duty. He had several deathbeds before he died, and never flinched on any. I remember in the Middlesex Hospital waiting, guiltily, for last words for a newspaper. For hours he had not moved, then came a faint stir.

"Brendan," I whispered. "Do you never think about death?" He sat up, like an enormous Pooh bear in a sheet like a toga. "Think about death?" he shouted. "Bigod, I'd rather be dead than think about death." It was an epitaph worthy of a permanent place in the *Oxford Dictionary of Quotations*.

There was also (though many may find it hard to believe) a shy, insecure Brendan who was worried and embarrassed by the headlines he could also command. If he was reluctant to write, if he began each new play with the author's curtain speech, this was not through arrogance or vanity. It was because he was deeply suspicious of his own talent, and sought continual reassurance of his abilities. He never believed what we critics wrote about him—but we were right and he was wrong.

I cannot think of anyone who has made me blush more in public. I never knew him as an intimate, but only a few close friends have ever given me warmer, richer, more lasting pleasure in private. The anaemic veins of the British theatre will be thinner and poorer for the loss of his 100 proof spirit.

NOTE

Alan Brien, English drama critic. See his review of *The Hostage*, "Political Pantomime", *The Spectator* (London), CCI (17 October 1958), 513–14; and of *Richard's Cork Leg* in *Plays and Players* (London), XX (November 1972), 42–3.

3

The Man Brendan Behan

by TIM PAT COOGAN*

Bars of one sort or another played a large part in the life and death of Brendan Behan.

He first saw his father through the bars of a prison, or rather his father first saw him, because he was a babe in arms at the time; and his exploits as a result of his fondness for bars of another kind helped to make him a world figure.

Naturally his antics made him unpopular with some sections of his countrymen, but it should be remembered that he was a man who as a boy spent long Sunday afternoons learning to make bombs in Killiney, Co. Dublin, and the greater part of his impressionable adolescence in British jails surrounded by convicts.

It's difficult at this stage to say what posterity's verdict on his work will be. It seems likely, however, that empirical, torrential, heartwarming, brilliant, but slightly undisciplined as it was, it will have the unusual fate of failing to outlive the memory of the artist who created it. He was completely self educated in the broader sense and was a good French and Irish scholar.

I once heard him described as being "like a barrel of porter. Full of goodness, heady, not to be taken in excess and with sediment that should not be stirred up." It was an apt description.

He seemed to live by balanced excesses, never doing anything in the way or in the quantities that everyone else did things.

He liked swimming for instance and stayed in literally for hours until his body was often blue with the cold.

* *Evening Press* (Dublin), (21 March 1964), p. 9.

On the Aran Islands, where he was probably the most popular visitor they ever had, his popularity survived an incident on Kilmurvey Beach when he dashed past a group of bathing girls and plunged into the water stark naked saying "Close your eyes, girls, I'm coming through."

At Seapoint or at Killiney one remembers the great shaggy head bobbing about in the water, picturesque verbiage emanating therefrom, and crowds of small boys sitting around the extraordinary man when he lay on the sand afterwards. He seemed to love children and to be loved by them.

Although his general attitude towards authority was "If there's a government I'm against it," he had too much perception and charity in him to be truly bitter.

The only time I ever heard him speaking really venomously about anyone was the time Billy Morton brought over the Liverpool police band to Santry. He cursed the Liverpool police from a height that day—showing me a scar on his forehead which he said he owned to an encounter with Liverpool's police in his teens.

He had the true Dubliner's almost diseased clarity of vision when it came to summing up situations or characters. But with him part of this ability was wasted owing to his inclination to see a bookie's tout as a decent man because of his job, whereas a banker or a professional man was one despite his position.

Here lay his strength and his weakness. On the one hand his writing was like his slumland speech, fresh, uninhibited, strong and compelling. Despite the fact that on the night of *The Quare Fella*'s premiere in the Pike I heard critics say "Ah yes it's enjoyable all right, but it won't do. It's not a play," he was hailed as the saviour of the British Theatre.

In person he had that indefinable personal magnetism that is sometimes called "star quality". It makes news. It makes people pay to see, read or hear its possessor.

But this is what killed him. A heavy drinker, he was at first delighted by fame after the success of *The Quare Fella*. The adulation, the flocks of predatory journalists, the celebrity treatment by a country that had once imprisoned him, the thing got out of hand. As the novelty of changing, without changing himself, from being an impossible outsider to the arch insider of his decade, a man about whom it was a conversational necessity to be informed, started to wear off.

The public image not so very different from the private one gradually overwhelmed the man, who could at various stages discipline himself enough to go away to the West to write saying "the only thing a writer needs is sobriety—and a quiet room to work in".

The flood of new writing was overtaken by new stories about the writer "dropping pound notes all over the floor of the pub . . . and then he said—". . . , the court appearances, the increasing visits to hospital. The great Catherine Wheel of his life and talent was beginning to burn itself out. People began to shake their heads and say: "He'll kill himself yet," first unbelievingly but gradually with what we now know to be a prophetic accuracy.

Most Dubliners, even those who disliked him, felt saddened when they heard that he had died; the public image has been diluted with regret for a very lovable, wayward, talented man, who improved either in private or in public with acquaintance.

In private I found him first of all the man who repelled me by saying nasty things about my father, because he had been instrumental in locking up a friend of his in connection with a tommy-gun, and then attracted me each time we met subsequently for years afterwards, making atonement through some pleasant little anecdote about my father which he would have picked up somewhere, until I eventually came to have a liking and sorrow for him equally and strongly.

In public I found him to be the object of one of the two most unusual and spontaneous outbursts of applause I ever witnessed. This was at the conclusion some years ago of the film *The Quare Fella*, in which he was interviewed by Eamonn Andrews when the audience gave a terrific clap. The only other time I ever saw this happen was at the end of the film of Queen Elizabeth's wedding— a touch which poor old Brendan would have enjoyed uproariously.

NOTE

Tim Pat Coogan, Irish writer and journalist. His other writings on Behan include "In Defence of Brendan Behan", *The Irish Digest* (Dublin), LXXII (July 1961), 15–18 [Recollections]; and "Closing Time", *The Spectator* (London), CCXII (27 March 1964), 406 [Obituary].

4

Brendan Behan

by FRANCIS MacMANUS*

I remember Brendan Behan in the morning, as it were, of his writing life when the dew was still on him. He used to ramble in to see me in old Radio Eireann in the very late 'forties and early 'fifties with scripts of short stories and talks and once with a few pages of a play about a man who was condemned to death for boiling his brother. Mostly he was alone. Sometimes he had his half-brother with him or some boozing friend he had picked up in a cattle market pub before any of us were awake. Alone or in company, he let the whole place know with a hullabaloo that he had arrived. With his gap-toothed grin and his fat round-cheeked country-woman's face he looked utterly harmless, like an overblown cherub.

The uproar was part of the Behan game. He could be docile as any lamb and sober as any judge when we got down to the job of reading and discussing whatever screed he pulled in a ball out of his pocket. But there were always preliminaries—an anecdote or two with appropriate jack-acting, a reminiscence of his time in gaol or in France, where he joined the Foreign Legion a few times for a bed and a meal, only to opt out the next morning; or even a song.

Once he arrived with a dreadful looking web-like gash on his chest oozing blood behind the remnants of a belly-open shirt. On his way into town he had passed over Leeson Street bridge and, seeing a few youngsters cavorting in the canal, he had peeled off his clothes and dived in to cool off; an old rusty broken bucket had met his chest. It took a lot of shouting and argument before he would let me apply an antiseptic. On another occasion he barrelled in with his mop of hair shiny and stiff like a gorgon's wig of hiss-

* The *Irish Press* (Dublin), (4 April 1964), p. 6.

ing angry snakes. What had happened was that on his way down Granby Row—Matt Talbot country—he had found a man varnishing a door, demanded to see his union card, discovered he had none, lumped him in with Matt as a non-union man and tossed the can of varnish up in the air for the sake of the solidarity of the workers.

What goes up must come down. It came down on Behan's own head. By the time he reached my office the varnish had stiffened and he was nearly weak with hilarity. He called it Matt Talbot's revenge.

Hilarity often enveloped him in a gale. Friends were greeted with fusillades of perfectly amicable four-letter words. Girls of every age and shape were kissed. Once in his more rotund days I saw him pretending to buss a very stout, good humoured lady. Their equators prevented conjunction. "The spirit is willing," he shouted, "but the flesh is in the way." He knew that she knew that he was playing the Behan Game. She was part of the conspiracy, a member of the cast.

Meaningless expletives were only part of the game. They had nothing to do with Brendan Behan the writer who, to use Coleridge's distinction, had an abundance of genius and very little talent. Talent is what puts the scaffolding up and the cement on the bricks. It's genius that conceives the building to send it soaring.

And Behan, as I flatter myself for having perceived so early, had genius as a writer. In 1953 I told an English class in the University of New York that an Irish writer they must look out for, as a genius, was Brendan Behan. If I were as lucky with horses I'd be a millionaire but then how many horses have been like him?

Amongst other things, he did two short stories for Radio Eireann that were full of the genius and of the newness and freshness of it, as close to the truth as pain to a wound, full of Dublin gurrier speech, transformed by feeling and rhythm and vision into poetry, and shaped with the roundness of the much told tale. I think they may be read in his book about Ireland. Maybe he had told and retold them. On paper they were alive. Over the microphone in his halting speech and strong accent, they were authentic with a life that had never been revealed before, except for a laugh. He could have been a great short story writer, speaking for a Dublin Joyce knew only by nocturnal adventure or guesswork.

But the craft was too lonesome for him. From beginning to end it meant quietness, solitude, working alone to discipline without an audience. I'll never forget how lost and alone he looked one day when, on receiving the red light signal in the studio, he failed to go ahead. When I went in to see what was wrong, he lifted his head, shaggy and jowled like the head of a battered Roman emperor and stammered, "I'm not feeling too good. I can't let you down." He was falling into a sort of mild coma. It was a warning of that disease which at last helped to carry him off. And remembering how it had carried off my own father as a young man, I nearly wept for him as for a doomed brother.

He was like a doomed brother a few weeks before he died when he came into Radio Eireann to see the Productions Director, Micheál Ó hAodha, and myself. Both of us felt that he was making his last rounds and that he was conscious it was the last. He sat in an old armchair and for nearly an hour told us a story about an adventure he had had in New York. In his good days he would have told that story in a few minutes, a gale of words, with mimicry, gestures, splurges of good-natured abuse and obscenity, but here at the last he took a slow hour, groping in long silences for the words, the memories, that seemed to elude him down ever-receding caverns. Several times we tried to help him by suggesting words to him and every time something of the old fire flashed up, the old volcano erupted. "Don't be putting words into my mouth," he raged. "Who's telling this story?"

He always told his story in his own way, precisely in his own way, and that was his genius. In his own way he wanted to give rather than to take. Did he die too young? Who can say? Perhaps he felt that he had given what he had been created to give.

Beannacht Dé len a anam.[1]

NOTES

Francis MacManus (1909–1965), Irish writer and member of the Irish Academy of Letters; became Director of talks and features in Radio Eireann in 1947.

1 *The blessing of God on his soul.*

5

He Was So Much
Larger Than Life

by FRANK O'CONNOR*

I remember the day I was first conscious of knowing Brendan
Behan. It was outside the Four Courts and a dishevelled-looking
tough said, "I know you. I saw you once with Kavanagh. What the
hell are you doing here?"

"I'm on a jury," I said. "And you?" "Oh, giving evidence for a
fellow that's up for pucking a Guard. I only got out of gaol this
morning. But he's a civil servant. He has to defend himself."

I got away from him for fear he might take the notion of pucking me instead of a Guard, but a couple of hours later I met him
again.

"Well, how did you get on?" I asked. "Ah, I only told the oul'
Judge what the Guard said to us, and what I said to the Guard
before I pucked him, and he said 'Oh, don't continue, Behan!
That's quite enough! We can take the rest for granted'." Soon
after, a Dublin solicitor with more imagination than lawyers
usually show, pleaded that Brendan's system was upset by the
sight of a Guard's uniform.

I cannot say I really liked him until after the arrest of Alan
Simpson[1] for the production of *The Rose Tattoo*. A little group
of us were waiting outside the theatre for the arrest of the cast—
a handful of theatre lovers, some newspaper men and a lawyer or
two, came to see fair play.

Brendan had managed to get a box and was delivering a long

* *Sunday Independent* (Dublin), (22 March 1964), p. 7.

speech in which he said quite truthfully that the country was being depopulated, and all the Government could do was to prose-
cute a harmless company of actors. Then he sang "Se Fath Mo
Bhuartha" with real feeling. The goat, which was a principal
character in *The Rose Tattoo*, emerged on to the lane, and he
shouted: "Never mind the goat! Bring out the —— peeler!"

He sent up to Mooney's at the bridge for a dozen of stout and
distributed it among his audience, saying, "Mind the bottles!
They'll come in handy for ammunition." I enjoyed watching
Brendan's glowing face, and later he and I went off for a drink
together. I remember thinking, "That man is twice life-size."

Later I read *The Quare Fellow* and reviewed *Borstal Boy*[2] and
was astonished again, because under that turbulent exterior there
was quite clearly the soul of an altar boy. I described *Borstal Boy*
as a deeply edifying book because the impression it left on my
mind was of someone who, like Mangan, was condemned "to herd
with demons from hell beneath" and who had emerged with his
essential purity and sweetness intact. Later, I noticed that even in
Dublin, where no one's reputation is safe, people everywhere told
stories of his goodness as freely as of his wildness.

A doctor who was attending him described how he would be
rung up by the Guards in the middle of the night and have to bail
Brendan out, but by the following evening Brendan would be on
his doorstep with apologies and the bail money. Someone else
told how he cashed a small cheque from Radio Eireann, then
bought a bottle of port and gave a shilling to a small boy to take
it to the house of a sick woman.

The same doctor described two old men with cancer who had
shared a ward with Brendan and were still alive, six months after
they should have been dead, waiting for him to call and cheer them
up with his songs and funny stories.

A poet described how Brendan had left him outside a house to
pay a call and how when he entered the house a half hour later he
found Brendan sitting by the bedside of an old woman in her last

agony, singing in a low voice to her with tears streaming down his face.

One heard the other sort of story as well, of course: the poet described Brendan later, beating his head with his fists and shouting: "Why should a —— like me be left alive and a grand woman like that die?" But he added: "That was Brendan putting it on; there was no put-on about the man I saw singing by her bedside."

It was the goodness people remembered about him. He wasn't only twice the size of life, but it was our life that he enlarged —the things we enjoy and value. It was curious to think that when we were trying to present to the world a sophisticated, prissy view of ourselves the man who represented us best was forever in gaol or hospital.

It was a disaster that he could not have had some success at home such as he later had abroad. With literary friends like Benedict Kiely and Francis MacManus, he did not have to apologise for the altar boy in himself, but theatre directors and censors could not see it. He was bitterly hurt by the banning of *Borstal Boy*, but for a reason our censors would not understand.

"The people whose opinions I care for", he said, "are simple people who can be taken in by fools like those. What can they think except that I'm a bad man?"

It left him open to the flattery of England and America, and I am afraid he vulgarised that small, pure, absolutely genuine gift of his, or allowed it to be vulgarised. I took care not to see or read *The Hostage* because dramatic critics in Ireland and America recognised it as a jazzed-up version of a story of mine,[3] and I did not want to see my work travestied by an English producer.[4]

It was typical of Brendan abroad that in that silly book *Brendan Behan's Island* he gave a false account of how he came to write it. In a Dublin pub he put on no such airs. "Ah, sure, of course I stole the —— thing."

I wish I had it in my power to suppress *Brendan Behan's New York* with which we are threatened.[5] It will not be New York and it will not be Brendan. I should be happier to think that some young writer was gathering up the hundreds of stories about him

32

that are circulating at this moment in Dublin and that would tell
scholars and critics a hundred years from now what sort of man
he was and why he was so greatly loved.[6]

NOTES

Frank O'Connor, pen-name of Michael O'Donovan, Irish novelist.

1. Alan Simpson, Irish theatrical producer who presented the world premiere of *The Quare Fellow* in Dublin in 1954. See his *Beckett and
   Behan and a Theatre in Dublin* (London: Routledge and Kegan Paul,
   1962).
2. Frank O'Connor, "To Show That Still She Lives", *Chicago Sunday
   Tribune*, (1 March 1959), p. 3.
3. "Guests of the Nation."
4. Joan Littlewood.
5. *Brendan Behan's New York*. With drawings by Paul Hogarth (London:
   Hutchinson; New York: Bernard Geis, 1964).
6. There are now two such collections: Sean McCann, ed. *The World of
   Brendan Behan* (London: The New English Library, 1965); and E. H.
   Mikhail, ed. *Brendan Behan: Interviews and Recollections* (in the press).

6

The Quare Fellow

by IRVING WARDLE*

Long before Brendan Behan died last Friday it was obvious that success had destroyed him, and in the macabre comedy of his final years he had the appeal of a "wild Dublin character" giving a repeat performance of the death of Dylan Thomas. At least he escaped the alien oxygen tent to die on home ground.

Behan was ill-equipped by upbringing to take care of his talent. His working-class childhood, with its motto of, "If you've got it, spend it," followed by his war-time imprisonment for I.R.A. activities, left him without any habit of self-discipline as a writer; and after *The Quare Fellow* he never wrote except for money. But on the strength of *The Quare Fellow* alone his is assured of a permanent place in the English-speaking theatre. This is what he will be remembered for, rather than for having perpetuated the myth of the stage Irishman in his over-publicised life.

Easily the finest play to come out of Ireland since Sean O'Casey's *The Plough and the Stars*, it has a prodigious richness of language, and an undiscriminating range of human sympathy which extends to the Mountjoy warders as well as to the prisoners; and by ignoring petty targets it rises to a passionately humane attack on the degradation of the prison system itself.

None of Behan's other works preserves this element of Swiftian indignation—perhaps because the direction of his talent lay too much towards anarchic comedy. *The Quare Fellow* was an uncharacteristically naturalistic work: in *The Hostage*, his most popular play, he broke down the theatrical categories altogether, using an I.R.A. incident for an extravaganza combining melodrama, farce, fantasy and ballad opera.

Perhaps the inspired chaos of the result was intended as a mirror

* The *Observer* (London), (22 March 1964), p. 24.

image of modern Irish nationalism. Or perhaps Behan's obsessive use of Irish Socialist–Republican themes after his own withdrawal from the movement was merely an index of his own contradictory blend of reverence and contempt for the past—a type of negative patriotism comparable to John Osborne's. The play itself leaves the question open—and it can be all too easily taken simply as a jolly Irish party.

Behan's autobiographical *Borstal Boy* and the subsequent book-making exercises that appeared under his name give few hints of how he might have developed. The waste is incalculable.

NOTE

Irving Wardle, English drama critic. See his review of *Richard's Cork Leg* in *The Times* (London), (20 September 1972), p. 7.

PART TWO

Brendan Behan the Writer

1

The Bloodshot World
of Brendan Behan

by RICHARD A. DUPREY*

The most disturbing thing about the Rabelaisian denunciations of
Brendan Behan, as he squints at us through bloodshot eye, is that
much of what he says is true. We dwell in a bawdy-house of our
own making—a society full of cacophony and disputation—
hypocrisy and cant. Though the ideals and high purposes of a
Christian life are as valid as they were in the days when Christ
walked the earth, our execution of them might utterly destroy the
patience of anything less than Divinity.

Brendan Behan, born in erupting Dublin in 1923, is a disturbed
child of the modern world. Taking up the bomb as a way of life
in his thirteenth year, Behan spent most of his life popping in and
out of jail like a jack-in-the-box, meanwhile writing and chatter-
ing about like an enraged hornet and getting as marked a reaction
from the world he stung. Only in the relatively mellow period of
his thirty-eighth year is he becoming sedate enough to savor the
life of a literary man.

Popularly known to the American public for his boozy ramblings
in theatres where his plays are done and through his comparatively
mild philosophising on television's "The Jack Paar Show", Behan
has become known as a sort of Gaelic clown-prince, a rambling
ambassador of the new Irish-Bohemianism. Nothing could be
further from the truth. In his autobiographical *The Borstal Boy* and
his two rather dissimilar plays, *The Quare Fellow* and *The Hostage*, Behan has set a good many tongues wagging with the violent
ribaldry of his pen. His works are stuffed with four letter words,

* *The Critic* (Chicago), XX (December 1961–January 1962), 55–7.

blasphemy, blatant irreverence, and a gift for controversial state-ment along with an undeniable poetic sense.

People who witnessed the play, *The Hostage*, laughed till they cried, later screamed to high heaven that the play should be shut down by the law, and then lived to be haunted by the violent crudeness of Behan's denunciations and, of course, their relevance. Behan is a social critic who uses blasphemy for a purpose, a pole-micist with a bag full of bombs. This is hardly surprising from a man who carried cordite and T.N.T. as the playthings of puberty.

Though he has frequently been attacked on artistic grounds after the moralists have spent themselves in righteous indignation, Behan is remarkably valid as an artist. Chalking obscenities on the out-house wall of the world, and the theatre does provide the world with such a facility. Behan represents a literal sort of neo-classi-cism which lives the Aristotelian analogy, crude as it is, that the theatre is a place of emotional defecation. However, rather than producing catharsis, Behan seems to indulge in it himself.

Behan is a nostalgic, sentimental man and surely this cannot be a surprise in any Irishman. The two great expatriates, Joyce and O'Casey, though far from O'Connell Street and the River Liffey, always betrayed a sad longing for the paths of their youth. Behan, who still walks the streets of his native city, between visits to "the pokey" and the United States, betrays a similar nostalgia for the innocence of youth . . . for the religious warmth of boyhood.

In *The Borstal Boy* he speaks in a surprising, sentimental way of serving Mass in an English reform school. He speaks of kneeling on the altar steps beside an English Catholic lad from the outside,

> . . . murmuring the responses and thinking of my mother sing-ing, "In that dread hour when on my bed I'm lying," while she rubbed hell out of the washboard, and of my grandmother, sneak-ing a pinch of snuff to her nostrils during the sermon in Gardiner Street, and of old Sister Monica, telling us to go asleep with our arms folded so that if we died during the night, we'd have a cross on us. I forgot everything but what I was doing.
> *Introibo ad altare Dei.*
> *Ad Deum Qui laetificat juventutum meam.*

In this reverie amidst exile, despite Behan's excommunication as a member of the Irish Republican Army and despite the brutalizing experience of prison and reform school, we see the petulant idealist who stands shaking his fist at God and country for not allowing him a better world.

We also see something in his attitude toward the Church as an open anti-clerical. In the violent interview described when the Borstal boy met the hard-hearted Father Lane, we see the sad human toll exacted by priestly uncharity, that rare and hurtful thing. The lonesome boy, hoping for warm priestly help, reacts violently to the cold hardness of the chaplain and as a mere boy finds himself incapable of seeing beyond the man and the place and the time. His reaction is naïve and childish but understandable in one young, alone and, for all his crust of defiance, afraid.

It is in this violent naïvete, so characteristic of rebellious children, that Behan's weakness lies, for with all his latent idealism, one can scarcely canonize petulance, and impatience is not to be confused with the theological virtue of hope.

The Hostage, the core offering of Behan's formal blasphemy, is an indictment of law, religion, home, country, human decency, art and even death—things that Behan, like all other men, loves or fears and at least respects. Despite a little *apologia* printed in the programme which denied that he reverences anything other than that which ". . . makes the roads safer, the beer stronger, or the old men and women warmer in the winter and happier in the summer," Behan shows himself the discountenanced dreamer, the irritated idealist, in the very fervour of his indictments. We are introduced to a world of tarts, pimps and homosexuals where there is, under the clever banter and song, a bitter mourning for lost innocence.

Strung on a flimsy thread of a plot, the characters philosophize, complain, yell at each other, and do self-consciously outrageous things to the utter, if somewhat carefully concealed, delight of the audience. It is a funny play but in the broader aspect of its form, it's the humour of a puny ant shaking his insect fist at the man who stands over him, with upraised and threatening foot. The ant cries out, "I'm not going to believe in you . . . I'll call you names! See how you like that!"

He rebels at everything. Not satisfied with a bevy of outrageous "queers", he names one of them Princess Grace. He has a whopping good time at the expense of the Irish clergy and while he's a bit less sly about it than James Joyce, he's no less outspoken. Even the theatre, here his chosen medium of expression, is given no quarter for he continually spoofs the form and causes theatre buffs to snort, "This isn't a play. It's vaudeville or burlesque!" There's an element of truth in this, of course, for the players dance, sing and engage in burlesque roughhouse.

Death too is brazenly funned at, but the jubilant jangling of "the bells of hell" strikes a note of falseness and in the shrill rejection of the young soldier's death at the final curtain—as he clambers to his feet to saucily trill at the audience, "The bells of hell go ting-a-ling-a-ling for *you* and not for me", one can see a hollow, schoolyard type of defiance flaunted in the face of the grim angel, Sariel. It is a defiance shown hollow in making the comparison to *The Quare Fellow*, the earlier Behan play. In that work, *jongleur* Behan plays "the Minstrel Boy" on a muted horn and there he shows a true dread of that day of wrath we all face.

The Quare Fellow, which at times plays like a tract, is a rather morbid depiction of the effects of an execution upon the inhabitants of a prison, convicts and guards alike. Illuminated only occasionally by flashes of gallows humour and now and then by vivid insights of the lonely and denuded state of men in jail, *The Quare Fellow* is more a self-pitying pamphlet than a play.

To be sure there is validity in Behan's discussion of capital punishment for he seems to feel with John Donne and Walt Whitman that all men are diminished by the extinction of human life —a single human life. The brutalization of the inflictors of such punishment and the welling guilt felt by those who commit bureaucratic assassination makes *The Quare Fellow* an arresting piece of human psychology and an interesting sociological treatise, if something way short of genuinely good drama.

Behan's sympathy for his fellow creatures is immense. In all his work there seems to be a true love for the harlot, the coward, the old and the stupid. There is a love for the halt and the blind and the demented. Even the British are treated with a love and understanding a bit difficult to understand coming from a veteran I.R.A. bomber.

Behan's language is interesting. He gives definite indications of being well versed in Ireland's writers. There's a Joycean quality in much of what he writes as he juxtaposes incredibly shocking terms, the jargon of Catholic philosophy, and patches of lyric beauty. The combination is eminently well suited to the theatre. There is an essential conflict set up with the linguistic structure itself that seems almost to compensate for the relative *stasis* of his plotting.

As for speech patterns in his dialogue, both in the plays and the autobiographical work, there is rather to be expected evidence that his ear is good for both the patterns of native Irish talk and that of Britain in its several dialects. There is a great credibility, too, in the raw, profane talk of gaol.

In the freedom of Behan's language there is further emphasis of the fact that he stands forth with great ardour for the freedom of the human spirit. He is not likely as anarchistic as he may at times try to suggest, for one would expect a man who has spent more than seven of his thirty-eight years in prison, to be antagonistic to law in any form and to those who enforce it. We can suppose, however, that this seeming anarchy is a matter more of reflex than of conviction.

There are those among us who have no patience for Behan and his art. These would have us thrust him from the stage back into the "chokey"—the solitary cell of artistic muzzling. This is to be expected, for artists and prophets can never hope to be popular. The world is suspicious of mirrors. Perhaps the twisted mirrors of the sideshow and circus can be countenanced, for they can be laughed at when they show the lean as fat and the obese as emaciated. It's the true glass that rankles us, the one that magnifies every crack and crevice, in which all the sags and bags of mortality can be clearly seen. In the presence of such a mirror man takes out his hammer and swings it wildly. It is a little strange that we Christians whose heritage in the early days of Christianity was one of renunciation of the world, asserting that it is vile and depraved, should feel called upon to defend today's world from its defamers.

Those Christians who indignantly defend contemporary society against the Behans of the world give evidence that they feel with Voltaire's idiotic Doctor Pangloss[1] that this is the best of all possible worlds. This is not quite defensible in the light of historical Christian thought.

Looking for the kingdom of God in the smoky mirrors of hell is neither terribly original nor awfully shocking. Dante did an admirable job of this and it has represented a major technique for God-seekers since. The Flemish playwright, Michel de Ghelderode, talking of finding God through blasphemy, is not so shocking, for despite the shrill wails of the prurient and the easily shocked,

43

Christ is always to be found consorting with the sinners and out-casts of the world. The damning indictments of respectability as found in the works of Bloy and Bernanos should warn the sincerely searching artist away from the shoals of respectability where the waters are placid but shallow and the revolutionary ideals of Christianity lack manœuvring room. Many a great potential artist has foundered on these shoals.

No such fate awaits the chunky bark of Brendan Behan for he sails deep waters. Though he may never prove to be a major vessel, lacking draught, and though he may swamp someday on one of his defiant voyages, he navigates well and as he sails, blasphemously thumbing his nose at the heavens, over the bay of art, he proves that his arrogant nose has caught the scent of God's great sea beyond.

NOTE

1. The tutor in Voltaire's *Candide* (1759).

2

The Writings of Brendan Behan

by COLIN MacINNES*

There are artists whose public performance is so flamboyant—
Byron, Alfred Jarry or Erik Satie are examples—that their contem-
poraries, repelled or dazzled by the man, have failed to measure
his artistic quality. This has been the fate of Brendan Behan. The
ex-Borstalian, the rebel in trouble with two governments, the in-
terrupter of his own plays in London and New York, the drinker,
the singer, the "broth of a boy" persona, have been a gift to colum-
nists and the shame of those who expect of artists that their
loftiest aim be the Order of Merit (or its Irish equivalent if there
is one—as I hope there isn't). That Behan's writings have some
virtue is allowed—but of what kind is it? For in all assessments
I have read of writing in English in the past decade, while significance is bestowed on many a dullard whose productions are
deemed, by the critical investigator, to conform to the "trend" or
"pattern" he discerns, the name of Behan somehow gets forgotten. This surprises me, for of all the writers of my generation, including myself, the only one who I am certain will be read a century
from now, is he.

Or rather, this does not surprise me; for the reasons that make
the unwary undervalue his achievement are so evident. Chief of
these is that he's an Irish writer. Now towards Irish writers (by
which, for the moment, I mean writers in English of whatever
race and faith who have drawn their essential strength from Ireland)
we have a divided attitude. We can admit, as we must, that without them "English" writing of the past and present would lose
half its weight. Yet we also seem to believe a benevolent magic
makes it so easy for Irishmen to be fine writers, that this gift of
nature deprives them of true merit. To be Jonson or Johnson or

* The *London Magazine*, II (August 1962), 53–61.

Daniel Defoe is the consequence of worthy labour. To be Congreve or Swift or Sheridan . . . why, they had only to loosen their delightful Irish tongues, and out it all came pouring like a blackbird's song! Shaw, Wilde, Synge, Joyce, O'Casey—they had only to talk, as in a trance, and the accumulation of generations of sweet grog-shop blarney (sufficiently transmuted by these writers to be artistically acceptable across the Irish Sea) came tumbling out to dazzle us; but we saw through the trick and, while bewitched, refused to bestow the severer kind of praise that Englishmen reserve for work manifestly resulting from qualities of character, labour, scholarship and earnest moral purpose.

I exaggerate, of course; but wish to suggest this patronizing attitude to Irish writing, largely unconscious and totally detestable, has as its basis—even in the most enlightened English minds —a political motivation. All our obsessions with India, Africa, Suez, Cyprus and the Caribbean, and the rights and wrongs of what we did and do there, serve somehow to mask from ourselves the fundamental fact of English social and political history, which is our centuries' old war with Ireland. It strikes me as significant, for example, that while dozens of Irish writers (including, of course, Brendan Behan) have found in this theme the chief material of their creations, not one English writer, so far as I know, has tackled it on the scale that it deserves. *A Passage to India* or *Mr Johnson* may not be profound analyses of the Anglo-Indian or Anglo-African disputes, but at least they are gestures, by Englishmen, in the right direction. But what English study have we of those centuries of bloodshed and oppression nearer home?

Having failed in this task of self-assessment—as much in our national thinking as more particularly in our writing—we have fallen back, in both these areas of consciousness, on the negative device of patronage and denigration. The Irish (without whose labour force, even today, our armies, hospitals and transportation system would collapse) remain worthy and slightly comical; and Ireland (whose dreadful division is exclusively an English responsibility, however much we try to hide behind the Orange lodges) a place of rapture and futility. We have forgiven the Irish for all the crimes we have committed on them; and the nastiest form this charitable gesture takes is to refuse to look Ireland in the eyes. Failing to do so saves us from the pain accompanying genuine repentance; but it also inhibits national self-knowledge, for until we have understood what we have done in Ireland, and are doing yet, we shall never understand ourselves.

The masterpiece is *The Quare Fellow* but I shall begin, chronologically, with *Borstal Boy*. As is by now well known, this describes Behan's arrest, imprisonments and final liberation (that is, expulsion) when, at the age of sixteen during World War II he attempted, as a volunteer of the I.R.A., to set off a bomb in Liverpool.

English legal convention, even in time of war, does all it can to deny the existence of political acts against the state, and seeks to reduce these to a criminal level. (A recent example is denial of the claim by nuclear disarmers now serving eighteen-month sentences, to a political rather than a criminal trial.) This makes the political prisoner's lot both worse and better. Worse because in countries where political acts against the State are recognised as such, their terms of imprisonment are more rigorous than for criminals (who are often appointed, as they were in Nazi Germany, official tormentors of the politicals); but better because, when treated by his captors for what he is, the political prisoner has at least the recognition of his higher moral status. At Behan's trial (despite that the police had treated him as a political by trying, unsuccessfully, to offer him freedom if he turned informer), the judge made it clear it was the bomb, not Behan's motives for its possession, that interested him: and this at a time when 200,000 men from the Irish Republic were voluntarily defending the English State, in its armed forces, by hurling bombs at England's enemies (or more exactly, at that moment, having bombs hurled at them). Behan's finest achievement as a man—or boy as he was then—was to have insisted, from the moment of his arrest until his expulsion, that whatever the laws and prison practice of the English might ordain, he *was* a political prisoner; and to have succeeded, with no force but his courage and personality, in making his captors treat him, in fact if not in law, the way he wanted.

The whole attitude of the Irish patriot to England—motives we can understand well enough, it seems, in Indians or Africans, but not yet, even today, in Irishmen—is the chief theme of *Borstal Boy*. Yet though I do not think Behan could be described as a "forgiving" person, his amazing triumph, as a man and an autobiographer, is to have given the English at every possible point—

47

and even in the most appalling circumstances—their human due. He is the best, the only real patriot—a man whose love for his country never denies the love others have for theirs, or fails to respect this love. And the portraits of English fellow prisoners, screws, and coppers is unfailingly sympathetic, whenever sympathy seems possible at all. Also, the English temperament, even when its manifestations most repel him (and make his life a misery) is entirely understood by an intelligent imagination. I am not sure how long after his first imprisonment Behan wrote *Borstal Boy*, but even supposing a maturer Behan bestows on his younger self a greater wisdom than he then possessed, there can be no doubt the Irish boy he was did win, by his humanity, an astonishing moral victory over his captors. This was possible because he is so clear-headed about himself: indeed in many ways, the most satirical portrait in the book is the one the writer draws of the young Brendan.

The language of *Borstal Boy* dispels another illusion about "Irish writing". The hackneyed convention is that the Irish are beguiling chatterboxes; and of course, Behan knows very well this is expected of a "Paddy", and turns on the blarney at times to amuse his captors (and divert their ire) or, more usually, to trick them and take the mickey. But the overall style of the book, though eloquent and passionate, is trim and lucid. Short scenes, portrait vignettes, swift emotional developments, are conveyed with admirable economy. From the first and final pages:

> Friday, in the evening, the landlady shouted up the stairs: "Oh God, oh Jesus, oh Sacred Heart. Boy, there's two gentlemen to see you."
>
> I knew by the screeches of her that these gentlemen were not calling to inquire after my health, or to know if I'd had a good trip. I grasped my suitcase, containing Pot, Chlor, Sulph Ac, gelignite, detonators, electrical and ignition, and the rest of my Sinn Fein conjuror's outfit, and carried it to the window. Then the gentlemen arrived.
>
> A young one, with a blonde, Herrenvolk head and a B.B.C. accent shouted, "I say, greb him, the bestud."

Then:

> "Passport, travel permit or identity document, please," said the immigration man beside me.
>
> I handed him the expulsion order.

He read it, looked at it and handed it back to me. He had a long educated countryman's sad face, like a teacher, and took my hand.

"Cead mile failte sa bhaile romhat."

A hundred thousand welcomes home to you.

I smiled and said, "Go raibh maith agat."

Thanks.

He looked very serious, and tenderly inquired, "Caithfidh go bhuil sé go hiontach bheith saor."

"Caithfidh go bhuil."

"It must be wonderful to be free."

"It must," said I, walked down the gangway, past a detective, and got on the train for Dublin.

I call Behan a poetic writer (and can offer no higher praise) not only because of his frequent quotations of Irish folk and political verses (the reverse of intrusive, and always heightening the dramatic or emotional effect), nor even because some of these verses are written by himself, but in the truer sense that his prose and poetry are almost the same thing; and that his prose, even in passages of factual description, is sustained by a vision which interprets fact imaginatively in evocative speech. This is never "poetic" in a lush purely verbal sense—and in fact, the more one reads Behan the more one is persuaded this rhetoritician has a classic sense of harmonious order, an almost severe self-discipline. Drama, though charged with feeling, is conveyed nearly with austerity. When Brendan hears that Charlie Millwall, his former Borstal "china" and an English sailor, has died at sea, he tells us the weight of his sorrow so obliquely that the passage, taken by itself, seems almost heartless. He speaks to the warder:

> I said nothing but "Thanks for telling us, Mr. Smith, and thanks for the bit of snout."
>
> "That's all right, Paddy, boy," said he, patting my shoulder.
>
> I went on up the road to the camp site and did sod all for the afternoon but drank tea with the plumber's head boy, which he made on his charcoal burner. And I gave him some snout and we smoked and drank tea and I listened to him telling me what he was done for, and how he was done, and I wasn't minding a word of what he was saying, or giving a fish's tit about him, or what he was done for, either, but saying, "yes" and "no" and "go on".

If I have hitherto left out the comedy—for which Behan, the "roaring boy", is most renowned—it is because, although this is hilarious (the cliché "makes you laugh out loud" is unavoidable), I see Behan as a tragic artist. I do not think it has been generally noticed that in his three published works a tragic death is the key event on which the whole drama turns. It may seem absurd to suggest one can miss this in *The Quare Fellow* which is, after all, about a hanging. But we never see this, nor even its victim, and the first impression left by the play of sardonic humour and abounding life is so overwhelming, that one almost forgets these arise from the fact of the man in the condemned cell. Likewise in *The Hostage*, though Leslie Williams is shot on stage just before the final curtain, the recollection of a comedy remains. (But of course, true comedy often is like this. The suicide at the end of *The Seagull* seems almost an irrelevance when it happens; but in retrospect, one can see the whole plot pivots round it, as *The Hostage* does round Leslie Williams's almost casual end.) In *Borstal Boy*, Behan is so discreet about Charlie Millwall's death that one may fail to realise, earlier on, exactly why it is that Charlie is almost stealing the book from Brendan. But in fact this death—described in less than a page—underlines how young Brendan loved this boy so much; and —even more vital to his whole political theme—how it is that Behan, risking death in his battle against England, can love and understand the very men his conviction forces him to try to kill.

Considered as a study of prison life the book is no less outstanding. The two prime features of this hateful existence any writer who knows it has got to evoke with some sort of objectivity, are the constant obsession of the victims to preserve their humanity amid perpetual authoritarian violence, and the form life takes when men are forced to live exclusively among men. Behan spares us nothing of the degradation prisons force on everyone inside them (on the screws even more than on the prisoners), yet his demonstration of how the instinct for life survives this test is beautifully conveyed without personal rancour. The sexual aspect is treated with humanity and tact: the inevitable homosexual element is introduced without undue mockery or morbid preoccupation, and the animal lives of the prisoners given a dignity snatched from every official effort to destroy it. The finest achievement is to have evoked love men have for each other without any of that nervous scruple with which a heterosexual writer—in dread of being thought by his readers to be otherwise—usually confronts this theme—or fails to do so.

50

Brendan Behan survived this prison ordeal (and others to come later) and can write so finely about it not only by the force of his own temperament (which seems to me prodigious), nor just because he was sustained by political belief, but as much because, even as a boy of sixteen, he was a highly educated man. It is clear from his language, his knowledge of history and politics, his easy familiarity with literature of books and, more vital, songs, that he enjoyed the blessing, as a boy, of a literate family in the most real and positive sense. And if his university was the North Circular Road in Dublin, one can only conclude, from what it taught him—that is, to be a civilised man who could win the respect and affection of illiterate English boys and primitive police officers against all adversity—that he was lucky not to have gone to any other seat of learning.

In *The Quare Fellow* Behan confronted a theme of daunting difficulty. An exclusively male cast, a principal character who is never seen, a setting of unrelieved gloom. From these unpromising materials (or, of course, being the artist he is, because of them) Behan has made a drama that is funny, humane, and a profound affirmation of the life that everything in the prison is trying to destroy.

The play opens with a song (and closes with a variant of it):

> A hungry feeling came o'er me stealing
> And the mice were squealing in my prison cell,
> And that old triangle
> Went jingle jangle,
> Along the banks of the Royal Canal.

Behan has been criticized for his addiction to incidental songs in his plays—in my view quite mistakenly (though perhaps his own occasional contributions from the stalls were somewhat excessive —but I do wish I'd heard them). It would seem that a people who once loved *The Beggar's Opera* (and to whom its modern transformation by Brecht and Weill is more or less acceptable) are embarrassed by the convention of mixed speech and singing, particularly in a "serious" play. I cannot account for this objection (or rather, don't want to bother to try to) if only because all theatre is in one sense illusion, and everything depends on the conviction

51

with which the artist uses any theatrical device. In *The Quare Fellow* Behan introduces song sparingly, with great tact and dramatic effect. From the outset, the very fact that an invisible prisoner is singing, and that the first character we see, a warder, stops him, establishes at once his central theme which is the conflict of life and joy with cruelty and death, and the triumph of life despite judicial murder:

> The screw was peeping.
> And the lag was weeping . . .
> *Warder:* The screw is listening as well as peeping, and you'll be bloody well weeping if you don't give over your moaning. We might go down there and give you something to moan about. . . . B Wings: two, three and one. Stand to your doors. Come on, clean up your cells there.

As we meet the prisoners and warders we are made aware that the forthcoming execution of the "quare fellow" is a shared obsession: the warders, the active party in the matter, being far more disturbed by it than the inmates. Snobberies, resentment and frustrations of the prisoners are conveyed with comic irony, reminding us that a jail population differs from that outside in no essential respect whatever. The first Act ends with an attempted suicide by a reprieved prisoner; and the dramatic effect of this, by bringing us so close to death so early, and by contrasting its "voluntary" nature in this instance with the irrevocable killing that must come, reinforces the gathering sensation of impending horror.

The central "character" of the second Act is the grave the prisoners are digging for tomorrow's victim: a riveting theatrical device, since the condemned man, though still unseen, becomes even more visible to the audience's imagination; and a device saved from the merely macabre by the intensity of feeling with which Behan invests this gruesome emblem, and by the speed and point of the sardonic dialogue he gives to the prisoners and warders who surround it. As time passes (by now we too are counting the hours till the execution) we meet in later Acts, and in increasing order of seniority, the hierarchy who are going to destroy this human life (and, by implication, meet the invisible judges, ministers and the society who have willed the deed). The warders at first seemed omnipotent, but now we see their Chief, their Governor and the

Hangman: an imported Englishman (since the "violent" Irish do not care, apparently, for this task) and, without doubt, one of the most revolting personages yet to be created by an English-writing dramatist. The one character we are drawn to is the young Gaelic-speaking warder Crimmin, who is as yet an innocent. It was a bold and characteristic device of Behan's to put the only really likeable man in the play among the oppressors, and he brings this off without a trace of sentiment or artifice. As the hour approaches, there are detailed physical descriptions by the prisoners of exactly what will happen to the quare fellow, so clinical as to be unbearable. Nervous tension rises, and the warders become openly the victims:

> *Warder Regan* (almost shouts): I think the whole show should be put on in Croke Park; after all, it's at the public expense and they let it go on. They should have something more for their money than a bit of paper stuck up on the gate.
> *Chief:* Goodnight, Regan. If I didn't know you, I'd report what you said to the Governor.
> *Warder Regan:* You will anyway.
> *Chief:* Goodnight, Regan.

As the clock sounds the hour, the prison is bedlam: warders and prisoners, locked in the same disaster, become indistinguishable, and the bars melt in the heat. The play ends with a brief and calculated dying fall . . . a life has been snatched, but life will go on forever.

Considered as a drama that soars from initial apparent *grand guignol* to authentic lyric tragedy, the play is beyond praise. Viewed as a demonstration that any alternative to judicial murder must be better—and, as forcefully, that prisons defeat their own supposed ends of humiliation or redemption—it will carry conviction to anyone capable of being convinced. Yet so fine is it as a play that, just as Greek tragedy haunts us still despite the moral mainsprings of the drama being quite different from our own, so I am sure *The Quare Fellow*, in whatever kind of social order that may replace our own, will never lose its human relevance.

We come out of jail in *The Hostage*—but only just so, since the central character, the young English soldier held in a Dublin house by the I.R.A., is again a prisoner. Despite its fateful ending, this is the gayest of Brendan Behan's works and the most overtly political. The Irish resentments of England, and their human sympathies for an Englishman, are beautifully conveyed by a houseful of comicals all sharply individual, not stereotypes. And for Behan, a man who has sacrificed so much for his political ideas, and who holds them so absolutely, it is brave not to hesitate to mock the sterile elements in Irish nationalism that he finds repellent. I think the fact is Behan is much more than an Irish nationalist merely—though he certainly is that: he is a revolutionary humanist, and his heroes belong to one nation of the socially oppressed in every country. This will be borne out even more specifically in his forthcoming *Brendan Behan's Island*—which will also contain the devastating satire on Anglo-Irish relations of his lunatic radio play, *The Big House.*

There remain two key elements in Behan's writing I must refer to, since I am sure of their importance, though with diffidence because of ignorance. The first is that he is an accomplished writer in Gaelic; and as I believe any writer who possesses two mother tongues is able to effect happy transmutations from the one speech to the other, this gift may help to account for the rich flexibility of his English prose. (Some of the African writers—for instance Chinua Achebe—can thus write impeccable English which is clearly enriched by the familiar possession of another tongue. And conversely, the "picturesqueness" that afflicts Synge's anglicized Gaelic may be due to his not knowing the native language.) The other element is the saturation of Behan's thought and speech by the spiritual inheritance of the Roman Catholic Church into which he was baptised. It is hard to tell from Behan's writings—which praise and castigate the Church with equal vehemence—how far he is what is known as a "believer". But that he has a religious instinct in the profoundest sense there can be no doubt; nor that his familiarity with Roman Catholic history, ritual and doctrine have contributed to his style and artistic temperament.

In the fickle "literary world" it is customary to deplore that Brendan Behan has not written more than he has. I shall not join in this impertinence if only because his life has been harder than most of his critics can imagine and, even more, because of the magnificence of what he has in fact achieved. All I feel I have a right to say is that I esteem his talent so highly, and admire so much what it has produced, that I hope with all my heart that we shall hear from him again.

3

Brendan Behan

by AUGUSTINE MARTIN*

Brendan Behan does not invite critical comment on his work. The whole character of the man discourages it. The public image that he has created is so tremendously alive and exuberant that one is inclined to regard the writing as a mere casual offshoot of his rollicking personality. As if, in fact, the work were there as an excuse to display the man. Again one feels a little silly in treating his work with more attention and respect than he allows it himself, tho' one wonders how he would feel if his audiences were to greet his productions as noisily as he himself does. He is not unique, however, in presenting this difficulty. Far from being original he could almost be said to be slavishly following a trail blazed by generations of his countrymen before him. It is almost necessary for Irishmen to detonate themselves in the centre of the field of English literature before they are noticed. (Of course the field gets wider and wider, hence the series of minor explosions as Mr. Behan recently progressed across the American Continent.) Others have chosen different methods. Wilde made his hit in America with considerably less achievement behind him than Behan—a slim volume of verse, a caricature by Gilbert and, of course, his genius. Shaw had to blow his trumpet loud and long in Hyde Park before the man and the drama grew to such for-midable stature. Then there was O'Casey's reverberating attack on James Agate, a gesture then tantamount to sacrilege. Behan falls into the same pattern, only his method is new. And all of them have presented the same sort of difficulty to the critic. The in-scrutable interpenetration of artist and work.

Nevertheless there are depths in Behan's plays that can only be reached by strenuous critical probing. In the midst of the wild

* *Threshold* (Belfast), No. 18 (1963), 22–8.

swirling words, the bizarre situations, the irreverences and the bawdy clichés of *The Hostage*, Behan's I.R.A. officer whirls on the convulsed audience and shouts: "Silence! This is a serious play!" And strangely, almost inexplicably the audience is made to feel that it is. That beneath the aggressive inconsequentialities there is a depth of human concern, a tragic core that is given point and dimension by being set against a background of gay slapstick degradation.

In fact Behan's world presents a level of human anguish and squalor that would be almost unbearable were it not relieved by his humour and compassion. His material is the people he knows best, the poor, the fallen, the degraded, the whole race of men that were born on the wrong side of the track. His youth and prison experiences have given him an insight to their souls and he is discerning enough to see the essential human innocence that lurked behind each mask. This spirit of innocence in the face of a seamy world emerges inexorably thro' all the obscenities of *Borstal Boy* rather in the way that Holden Caulfield's innocence emerges irresistibly thro' the profane idiom of Salinger's masterpiece. It is notably represented for instance by the characters of Leslie and Teresa in *The Hostage*, which I shall refer to later.

What is presented indirectly, symbolically, in *The Hostage* is seen in simpler, more naturalistic terms in Behan's earlier play *The Quare Fellow*. Here, as in *The Hostage* the central preoccupation is with death. A man, the "quare fellow" of the title, has killed his wife and the play deals with the way the other convicts in the prison fill in the time joking and speculating as they wait for his execution. The main character never appears but his presence and his fate haunt the entire action. At the outset it is just another execution—he had "killed the thing he loved" and he too must die; to that extent, his death is meaningful, the convicts don't question it. But as the play progresses it becomes a sombre backdrop against which the lives and aspirations of the convicts are thrown in all their sad meaningless horror. The following extract from a conversation between Dunlavin and Neighbour exhibits Behan's understanding of stark physical and mental discomfort:

> *Neighbour:* Only then to wake up on some lobby and the hard floorboards under you, and a lump of hard filth for your pillow, and the cold and the drink shaking you, wishing it was morning for the market pubs to open, where if you had the price of a drink

you could sit in the warm anyway. Except, God look down on you, if it was Sunday.

> *Dunlavin:* Ah, there's the agony. No pub open, but the bells battering your bared nerves and all you could do with the cold and the sickness was to lean over on your side and wish that God would call you.

There is no cant or sententiousness here; this is the razor-edge of human desolation, the moment between salvation and despair. But it never really reaches despair, because his people are fundamentally Catholic, exhibiting even in the depths of their discomfort and aberration a consciousness, however vague, of God and eternity and the hope of ultimate salvation.

As the play slowly progresses and the hope of reprieve fades, all the grim paraphernalia of death are presented. Only in flashes, as in the arrival of the chaplain, is it regarded by the characters in any of its awful reality. The Quare Fellow is criticised for failing to drop his cigarette ends for the other prisoners to collect; the digging of his grave is a welcome break in the convicts' routine, an opportunity for a smoke; the hangman arrives, a cheerful innocuous little man who sees the execution simply as a job to be done. The convicts speculate on the possibility of getting his letters and selling them to the Sunday papers; two of them lay wagers on his final fate. And finally the condemned man is hanged while one of the prisoners gives a running commentary on the execution in the parlance of a radio commentary on a horse race. The death has taken place and the grim unheeding life of the prison goes on. In their own apparently callous way the convicts, like the world, have averted their eyes. But Behan has ensured that the audience cannot easily do likewise. He has forced it on our attention and in the artistic terms of the play he has shown modern man, his criminal indifference to death and its appalling significance and finality. Perhaps this is the nerve in the contemporary public that Behan has hit and maybe it is this that accounts for his present celebrity. For he attacks the same problem in *The Hostage* and again he presents it in acceptable terms, forcing us to look at it under the illusion that we are looking at something else.

It is a curious fact that Behan's plays, which are much more daring and outrageous than O'Casey's and Synge's, have scarcely caused a murmur of protest when they were presented in Dublin. Perhaps Irish audiences have seen their essential seriousness, perhaps they have recognised the essential tho' carefully disguised innocence that I referred to above, perhaps they feel more kinship with the inherent Catholic consciousness that informs them. It must be remembered that all our great playwrights, Yeats, Synge, O'Casey, Wilde, Goldsmith, Beckett, have been in the Protestant tradition. In any case Mr. Gabriel Fallon has had this to say of Behan's work:

> He has merely taken life as he found it and constructed in his own terms with a facility, which at its highest point, amounts to genius. That he has done so to the annoyance of self-appointed moralists and professional patriots is, perhaps inevitable in this country which still cherishes a skin-deep supersensitiveness as its greatest virtue. Behan is not asking us for our laughter. Properly understood, he demands our understanding, our pity, our sympathy and—should we possess such a quality—our Christian charity.

This, to me, seems to get to the heart of Behan's elaborately concealed preoccupation. He wished us to see with the spirit of charity that whole region of agony, anguish and tragic absurdity that lurks at the darker frontiers of our world. (If there is an existentialist ring about these terms it is deliberate. Behan is more of a European than his Irishy act might suggest and it may be significant that Gabriel Marcel found *The Hostage* "deeply impressive".)

Hitherto we have seen this world imperfectly, thro' the distorting lenses of conventional cliché. Behan, especially in *The Hostage*, makes war on the cliché views of things, the theatrical half-truths that surround death, patriotism, religion, love. Here again a man is sentenced to death. In this case he is not guilty of any particular offence. He is a young English soldier called Leslie, and the I.R.A. have captured him as a hostage and intend to shoot him if one of their own men who has been sentenced to death is executed. He is imprisoned in a Dublin brothel where Behan has assembled a company of prostitutes, fanatics, perverts, and eccentrics. Here Leslie is forced to wait and listen to the songs, jokes, sententious posturings, religious and patriotic platitudes that Behan puts in the mouths of his characters and which he deploys in brilliant and hilarious juxtaposition. An innocent young servant girl called Teresa befriends him and these are really the only two characters on the stage. Everyone else is in varying degree the mouthpiece for some petrified and lifeless platitude. The mad Monsewer with his kilt and bag-pipes who thinks the "Troubles" are still going on; he is given that old song "The captains and the Kings" which he sings at a most incongruous moment, nostalgically recalling gracious Georgian days:

> By the moon that shines above us
> In the misty morn and night,
> Let us cease to run ourselves down
> And thank God that we are white,
> And better still are English
> Tea and toast and muffin rings
> Old ladies with stern faces
> And the captains and the kings.

There is the enigmatic Mulleady: "I'm a secret policeman and I don't care who knows it!" Miss Gilchrist the badly damaged religious fanatic, Pat the wounded veteran of the old I.R.A., the perverts Princess Grace and Rio Rita. This mad meaningless swirl of figures revolves round the bewildered Leslie who can scarcely grasp or believe the reality of his salvation. Eventually he is killed and the whirl momentarily stops, and Teresa is given one brief poignant speech over his body:

> . . . I will never forget him. He died in a strange land and at home he has no one. I will never forget you, Leslie. Never till the end of time.

It looks for a moment as if the play is going to dissolve in pathos, but this is the one thing Behan cannot allow. Instead he has Leslie jump up and lead the company in a final song. This ending has offended many critics. Mr. Sam Hynes in an interesting article in the American periodical *Commonweal* states the case thus:

> In the end the hostage dies a meaningless accidental death, and then hops up again to sing a comic song. The whole play oscillates between irony and pity: irony without purpose and pity without focus. But purposeless irony is a final denial of values and unfocussed pity is sentimentality.

This is clear and trenchant reasoning, if the premises are correct. But supposing Behan has a purpose beyond those gestured towards by Mr. Hynes! I suggest that Behan wants to demonstrate that there is essentially something meaningless and accidental about all political assassinations. That he refuses to treat death with the reverence of traditional drama precisely because modern man does not treat it with the reverence and pathos of traditional man. In other words he is not recoiling from or dismissing the fundamental significance of death but underlining and satirising a whole modern attitude, and his ending is really his master-stroke, the ironical twist that throws the whole play back into perspective. And finally the song Leslie sings is not so very comic really. It is an old song that goes:

> The bells of hell
> Go ting-a-ling-a-ling
> For you and not for me.
> Oh death where is thy sting-a-ling-a-ling
> Or grave thy victory?

The song, sung by the dead man, refuses to let the audience comfort itself with any sort of phoney pathos. It points out to us our fundamental indifference, the "I'm alright Jackery" exhibited by the world as represented on the stage. And ironically as the song ends the world goes on doing just that:

> If you meet the undertaker
> Or the young man from the Pru
> Get a pint with what is over
> Now I'll say goodbye to you.

In fact Behan thinks that death is important enough not to be clothed in clichés. Mr. Hynes claims that this is all "the tough con's refusal to expose himself to emotion!" I believe that is true, but it is by no means the whole truth.

I would therefore suggest that *The Hostage* is primarily a satire. It is not delicate nor indeed always successful satire. But it is not without reverence. It is not patriotism, religion or sex that he is attacking but rather the false attitudes we adopt towards them, the clichés in which we express these attitudes and in which all their falsehood is petrified and perpetuated. This is the purpose of all the songs and set speeches. These songs and speeches, couched in their appropriate clichés, are set against a background and a moment that exposes their fundamental falsehood and absurdity, the half-truths and the mushy sedatives that they dispense. This is Behan's method of shaking people out of their mechanised narcotic stupor. It is basically the method of Shaw and Swift and all the great satirists.

61

I am not claiming that Behan has already proven himself a great dramatist. His faults are all too obvious. He is often obscure, inclined to substitute vulgarity for wit, given at times to dreadful stage-Irishy both in dialogue and sentiment. He obviously finds great difficulty with construction and no one knows how great his debt is to Joan Littlewood in this respect. However, it cannot be denied that with her he has pioneered a new dramatic form in the modern theatre. His *Hostage* has been a great blast of fresh air blowing thro' contemporary drama, it has really been a cleansing influence, for Behan's sensibility is essentially robust and healthy. He has restored the belly-laugh to its proper place in serious theatre; it had been absent since the days of the great Elizabethans. This in itself is a very considerable achievement.

4

"This Dying Lark"

by TOM MacINTYRE*

The Behan story, in a way, begins with the Playboy riots of 1907. Irish nationalism, the Establishment-to-be, had fuelled (and, of course, was fuelled by) the new drama but Synge had dared to call a spade a shovel, and so rose the hullabaloo-clamorous reminder that, if there was to be theatre in Ireland, it must be theatre according to the rules. The O'Casey riots emphasised the point, and O'Casey's departure—granted his quarrel was more with The Abbey than the mob—was, in its consequences, an Establishment victory. Denis Johnston, through the '30s, was too hot for The Abbey to handle—The Gate Theatre gave him refuge. By the '40s, respectability had won: the writers had been driven from theatre to the comparative safety of the short-story and the lyric poem. Do you dare to write a play? Behan dared but, by now, the venue had to be London. Truth might flourish in Stratford E.15, but, in Dublin the blinds were down.

This then—the manner in which the stifling of a theatre is illustrated—is an important part of the story. There is, however, something more to be said: it may well be that Behan, with all his naked vitality, ultimately won. Censors cannot provide for everything. Even if he had to campaign from abroad, such was the brio of his gift that polite and politic Ireland shuddered—and in the shudder was undone: the spasm was irrevocable, charted. No Vance Packard is needed to detect that the island can never be the same again.

Borstal Boy (banned in Ireland yet)[1] was a tremendous opening salvo. Behan, who believed in no rule except the rule of love, saw no reason why he shouldn't commence with a volume of auto-biography. Perhaps he was, in any case, unable to imagine himself

* *Kenyon Review*, XXVII (Winter 1965), 152–55.

grave in years, and predictably turning to the genre then. He loosed the book. If the American critic who swore "One *Borstal Boy* is worth a dozen *Catchers in the Rye*" was overstating the case, I can understand that euphoria of discovery. The autobiographical vehicle was made for Behan: the swashbuckling life of the man could go on the rampage here, uninhibited by the formal demands of novel or story. (Maybe, for that matter, the form is made for the Irish: I think of Moore, O'Casey, O'Connor. It saves the whole bother of writing a novel, and if a kind of Jamesian *felt life* is what you're looking for—the authors seem to say—then, by God, here it's for you!)

Borstal Boy is fresh, authentic Behan: the humanity, the delicious bawdy, the insuperable zest of Dublin lane and alleyway, the swagger of Dublin tenement speech. Behan is in O'Casey country here, and it is a measure of the former's individuality that the notion of pastiche never inserts itself. The prose styles are quite distinct. While they share the enterprise and imaginative fling which mark the Irish use of English (and here I must lugubriously report that I.B.M. is moving in), the crisp expression of *Borstal Boy* is a long way from the rosy rhetoric of O'Casey.

If, putting down the book, you are still sufficiently sober to ferret for the flaw, it will likely be uncovered as a weakness typically Irish—a feeling intensity that is hard put to stop short of sentimentality. This has been the trouble, the catch, with Irish lyricism all along: the bladder is dangerously near the eye. Behan didn't altogether escape that, but what preserves him from its worst consequences is a sense of humour generous and foamy as a barrel of porter. Again and again it protects him in moments when a sentimental naïveté threatens.

The Quare Fellow: cometh the hour, cometh the man—or the woman. It would, of course, have happened anyway—Behan's vigorous and revivifying adventure in theatre—but the coincidence of Joan Littlewood's emergence, with her theatre workshop, was accelerating. At least to start with, here were the producer, the players, the theatre for a Behan play. *The Quare Fellow* had already been staged in the minute *Pike*, a club theatre, in Dublin but the greater freedom and resources of Stratford enhanced the piece immeasurably. The Littlewood doctrine is one of love and celebration, along with a strong belief that audiences ought to be drawn into the experience of theatre as much as possible. It implies a hell-for-leather spontaneity, and freedom to begin by throwing in the kitchen sink. Behan was game for anything. These were his sentiments, this his arena. Dublin, and the blighting eye of His Eminence, the Archbishop, must have seemed a million miles away.

> A Hungry feeling came o'er me stealing
> And the mice were squealing in my prison cell,
> And that old triangle
> Went jingle jangle
> Along the banks of the Royal Canal.

From the nipping and eager air of that opening to the chilling grotesquerie of the climax—Mickser's blasphemous commentary on the game, "We're off, in this order: the Governor, the Chief, two screws Regan and Crimmin, the quare fellow between them, two more screws and three runners from across the Channel, getting well in front, now the Canon. He's making a big effort for the last two furlongs. He's got the white pudding bag on his head, just a short distance to go . . ."—the play moves with the formless rigidity, forbidden laughter, and gaunt assurance of any prison day. Perhaps the perfection of its architecture is largely due to the poet in Behan which leads him to ride the rhythm—as in *Borstal Boy*— and let it carry him to the miracle that must be pending.

The acute social conscience the play reveals, and not merely in relation to the central issue of capital punishment, goes back through O'Casey to Jim Larkin, the Labour leader who, above all others, was the protector of Dublin's poor in the early decades of the century. O'Casey and Behan (the name of James Plunkett also suggests itself) hadn't the Parnell Joyce was blessed with but they had a Larkin—and passionately acknowledged it. "I was part of him, we were all part of him," says Behan in one of his Gaelic poems written on the occasion of Larkin's death in 1947.[2] Behan's constant tilting at the hypocrisy of priest and politician reflects the bitterness of strike and lock-out and meagre rations and wretched housing while, ermined or top-hatted, those in great place jaguared smoothly by.

In a variety of ways one can see *The Quare Fellow* as part of Irish drama: it *belongs*. There is the facet discussed above, there is the delight in characterisation almost for its own sake, there is the progress from broad extrovert humor to the uniquely pitched destructive gibe—the "senseless mocking laughter" which Shaw

accurately named, and so on. But *The Hostage* is another matter
entirely. It belongs to the Littlewood movement in British drama
of the '50s, and, like many a triumph of that movement, it spot-
lights a danger for your playwright when communal workshop
fervor takes over.

In this explosive charade, there is less of Behan than in almost
anything he wrote. The impetus is ferocious, the satire on Anglo-
Irish shenanigans irreverent and entertaining. Raffish and unfore-
castable, the shindy never sags but—no disrespect to the producer,
the actors, actresses, stagehands, and everybody else who had a
say—the absence of a dominating creative personality is irremedi-
able. *The Quare Fellow* did have that quality. It was plangent beneath the comedy, consistently audible and, by the climax, made a
howl in your viscera. There's an odd relevance in Behan's on-stage
jigacting during the London run of his second play: was he also,
by that time, a hostage?

The whole decline is further reflected in *The Hostage*'s lack of
a central character. *Leslie* needn't apply—maybe it was never intended that he should. *Monsewer* is zany caricature—neither will
he suffice. Any other offers? It would seem that Littlewood leger-
demain and panache were meant to carry the piece. And the
extraordinary thing is that these qualities *do* carry it quite a considerable distance. Nevertheless, when the hooley is over, I want to
know what has become of Behan? Are we to content ourselves with
glimpses? Behan, never a doubt of it, *was* The Quare Fellow, a man
waiting for the rope, and his protest at the horror of it gives the
feel of hemp about the throat. In *The Hostage*, he is diminished
by gimmickry. It is an iridescent kind of gimmickry, but the bullet
which kills Leslie leaves us unscathed.

An area of Behan's work about which very little is known outside Ireland is his achievement in Gaelic poetry. His lyrics, if not
numerous, are of high quality, and many of them, quite somber
poems with a dignity in their grieving, present a Behan not to be
found elsewhere. Here is the moan of the jester which we might
have assumed but seldom were allowed so openly to hear. His poem
on Wilde's death, "Jim Larkin", "A Jackeen's Lament for the
Blaskets", "Existentialism", and "Repentance" (the latter written
in jail with the needle given him to sew mailbags)—these are all
splendid, and show that his sensitivity in handling language was
not confined to English. It's interesting to reflect that, for his hours

of most personal utterance, he should have chosen Gaelic. Intensifying the privacy? Or did he simply prefer its resources in the lyric mode? Whatever the answer, I'm left with the feeling that in these poems his rumbustious spirit comes finally to rest.

"He ran too hard", was the humane, shrewd comment of O'Casey when he heard the news. Perhaps he did, but there was no other way. There was too much to do. Prudence he would leave to policemen and such. Meanwhile, he would cry the glory of the gallop, be it short or long. On the day of the funeral (the Establishment hovered by discreetly), a second, hardly noticed coffin lay in the mortuary chapel alongside Behan's. Not alongside either but well to one side, neglected, anonymous, lamentable. For that reduced brother, Behan would have had a glance, a word. Maybe, even at that moment, he was saying companionably (as when some Dublin Boswell quizzed him on the subject of death), *Ye know, I don't like this dying lark. I don't like this dying lark at all.* That was Behan, the man, the work.

NOTES

1. The ban was lifted in 1970.
2. Brendan Behan, "Jim Larkin", *Comhar* (March 1947).

5

The Quare Fellow

i. *The Quare Fellow* by Brendan Behan
by *A. J. Leventhal**

Brendan Behan is no expressionist but if he has contrived to write
a play, *The Quare Fellow*, with no recognisable form, he has,
nevertheless, produced a powerful piece of propaganda, as powerful
as his recurring recorded voice that sings out its baritone jingle-
jangle from a punishment cell with telling dramatic effect. There
can be no question as to the intensity of his implied plea for the
suppression of judicial hanging. His approach is not that of Charles
Duff (although he owes him something) who, in his *Handbook
on Hanging*, uses satire and statistics to arouse interest in the minds
of a normally apathetic public. Brendan Behan has obviously had
experience of life in prison and his sincerity in stressing the in-
humanity of capital punishment can be as little doubted as Oscar
Wilde's when he wrote his *Ballad of Reading Gaol*.

Throughout the three acts of the play the scene is set either
in the city prison or its exercise yard. We do not meet the "quare
fellow" who gives the play its title. He is the condemned man and
the author endeavours to maintain dramatic suspense by the reaction of the other prisoners to the possibility of his reprieve. The
interest in this rather carelessly made play is kept alive by the
vitality and the plausibility of the characters—prisoners, warders
and some hangmen. Sean O'Casey and Donagh MacDonagh have
mined the purlieus of the Liberties for picturesque speech and it
would have seemed that there were no fresh words to conquer.
This, however, is not so for Brendan Behan's dialogue is outstanding and his ear has caught and retained a rich Dublin modern slang
laced with a specialised lag lingo.

* *The Dublin Magazine*, XXI (January–March 1955), 47–8. This is a review
of the world premiere of the play at the Pike Theatre, Dublin, 19 November
1954.

For this alone we should be grateful to the Pike Theatre for producing the play. In it there is comedy as well as pathos and the
humorous parts were better sustained than the others. Pat Nolan
was particularly conspicuous in the crowded cast. Gearoid O'Loch-
lainn, as Warder Regan, who combined religion with a partiality
for drink, gave a good rendering of a complicated character. The
acting generally was adequate and the small stage failed to cramp
the inventive genius of Alan Simpson as producer.

* * *

ii. The End of the Noose by *Kenneth Tynan**

"Bloddy sparklin' dialogue", said a pensive Irishman during the
first interval of *The Quare Fellow* (Theatre Royal, Stratford, E15)
and sparkle, by any standards, it amazingly did. The English hoard
words like misers; the Irish spend them like sailors; and in Brendan
Behan's tremendous new play language is out on a spree, ribald,
dauntless and spoiling for a fight. In itself, of course, this is scarcely
amazing. It is Ireland's sacred duty to send over, every few years,
a playwright to save the English theatre from inarticulate glum-
ness. And Irish dialogue almost invariably sparkles. But now consider the context of Mr. Behan's hilarity. His setting is an Ulster
prison, and one of its inmates is shortly due to drop, rope-neck-
laced, through the untender trap.

To move wild laughter in the throat of death?

It cannot be: it is impossible.

But Berowne was wrong. To a countryman of Swift many things
are possible, and this among them; this, perhaps, especially.

In adversity, the Irish always sparkle. "If this is how her Majesty
treats her prisoners," said one of them, handcuffed in the rain
en route for gaol, "she doesn't deserve to have any." With this
remark of Oscar Wilde's Mr. Behan, who has spent eight years of
his life in prison for sundry acts of I.R.A. mischief, entirely agrees;
and his protest is lodged in the same spirit of laconic detachment.
The Irish are often sentimental about causes and crusades, but
they are hardly ever sentimental about human beings. So far from

* The *Observer* (London), (27 May 1956), p. 11.

trying to gain sympathy for the condemned man, an axe-murderer known as "the quare fellow", Mr. Behan keeps him off-stage throughout the action. All he shows us is the effect on the prison population of the knowledge that one of their number is about to be ritually strangled.

There are no tears in the story, no complaints, no visible agonies; nor is there even suspense, since we know from the outset that there will be no reprieve. Mr. Behan's only weapon is a gay, fatalistic gallows-humour, and he wields it with the mastery of Ned Kelly, the Australian bandit, whose last words, as the noose encircled his neck, were: "Such is life." Mr. Behan's convicts behave with hair-raising jocularity, exchanging obscene insults even while they are digging the murderer's grave. An old lag feigns a bad leg in order to steal a swig of methylated spirits; a newcomer anxious to raise bail is blithely advised to "get a bucket and bail yourself out." Even the hangman is presented serio-comically as a bowler-hatted publican with a marked addiction to the wares he sells. The tension is intolerable, but it is we who feel it, not the people in the play. We are moved precisely in the degree that they are not. With superb dramatic tact, the tragedy is concealed beneath layer after layer of rough comedy.

Meanwhile, almost imperceptibly, the horror approaches. Two warders, chosen to share the murderer's last eight hours of life, thoughtfully discard their wrist-watches in anticipation of his inevitable demand: What time is it? His last letters are thrown unopened into his grave: better there than in the Sunday papers. Dawn breaks, accompanied by the ghastly, anguished clatter of tin cups and plates against iron bars that is the tribute traditionally paid by the thousand convicts who will see tomorrow to the one who will not. The empty exercise yard now falls silent. The hush is broken by a unique *coup de théâtre*, Mr. Behan's supreme dramatic achievement. An unseen humourist, bawling from some lofty window, embarks on an inmaginary description, phrased as racily as a Grand National commentary, of the hundred-yard dash from condemned cell to scaffold. They're coming into the straight now; the chaplain's leading by a short head. . . . A young warder, new to the ceremony, faints and is carried across the stage for treatment. A sad, bawdy ballad filters through from the punishment block. The curtain falls, but not before we have heard the swing and jerk of the drop. I left the theatre feeling overwhelmed and thanking all the powers that be for Sydney Silverman.

John Bury's two sets exactly capture the aridity of confinement. And Joan Littlewood's production is the best advertisement for Theatre Workshop that I have yet seen: a model of restraint, integrity and disciplined naturalism. Glynn Edwards, Brian Murphy and Maxwell Shaw, as three of her Majesty's guests, and Dudley Foster, as one of the same lady's uniformed hosts, stand out from an inspired all-male company. Miss Littlewood's cast knows perfectly well what it is doing. She must now devote a few rehearsals to making sure that we can understand precisely what it is saying. That done, *The Quare Fellow* will belong not only in such transient records as this, but in theatrical history.

* * *

iii. O'Casey Goes to Jail by *Maurice Richardson**

Perhaps the first point to stress about *The Quare Fellow* (Theatre Royal, Stratford, E15) is that you do not need to be fervently opposed to capital punishment to appreciate it. This is an artistic not a propagandist triumph, and you could be as firm a believer in, or as practised an exponent of compulsory liquidation as, say, J. V. Stalin, Mr. Pierrepoint, or the Home Secretary and still have to admit that this is the hell of a fine play and that Brendan Behan looks like possessing all the attributes of a really considerable playwright.

It might be said that a hanging, with its curiously obscene ritual, exercises such a strong obsessional fascination that it makes a play all on its own; and that Behan, with the advantages of eight years' prison experience, had merely to write a faithful documentary. There is no doubt some truth in this, but there is more to *The Quare Fellow* than good reporting, to say nothing of the ingenious stagecraft. Out of a cast of a score or so nearly everyone came alive, and distinct. The dialogue crackled electrically and was never verbose. It fitted the acrid prison scene as naturally as O'Casey's fitted the tenements of Dublin's north side.

* *New Statesman* (London), LI (2 June 1956), 624–26.

The mood throughout is one of absolute realism with a strong sardonic tinge. The prisoners wisecrack and mutter quasi-obscenely and make joke after joke about "topping", just as prisoners do. The first act is set on a landing outside a row of cells. The characterisation here is one of the features of the play; it catches you like a whiff of Jeyes Fluid soon after the curtain rises. Three in particular establish themselves. The first is Dunlavin, an excellently goatish clown of a type which the *lumpenproletariat* of Dublin or Liverpool is constantly throwing up. He was cleverly played by Brian Murphy who made him skittish and tough with the right hint of epicenity. The second is a hefty great housebreaker, a very satisfactory performance by Glynn Edwards despite some difficulty with the Irish accent. The third, an ageing, villainous and probably tabetic cripple might almost have stepped out of the *Walpurgisnacht* scene in *Ulysses*; he was rendered obscene, mean, salivary and very human by Gerard Dynevor.

One of the two murderers in the prison, a middle-aged wife-killer who has just been reprieved, is brought in from the condemned cell to start his life sentence. His reception by the others, with its rough kindness—about as rough as a sink scrubber—and total tactlessness (for instance, some of their remarks when swarming round the window trying to get a glimpse of the women prisoners over the way) is, you feel, utterly right.

The rest of the play is staged in the exercise yard on the eve of and during the hanging. The problem of letting us see enough of the prisoners is solved, neatly enough, by having a working party digging the Quare Fellow's grave. Inevitably the prison staff begin now to occupy the centre of attention. Behan allows two out of his four screws to be men of more than average kindness and sensitivity. Even his bibulous English executioner (overdone? I wonder) is a cosy comic, and all the more sinister for being so. We never see the condemned man. After much ingenious manipulation of tension nearly everything that happens—apart from a fainting warder being carried out—happens off-stage. A prisoner's voice, from a cell window high up, gives a mock running race commentary on the walk to the scaffold. We hear the drop, a muffled downbeat. The climax is the roaring jangle of protest as the prisoners rattle and bang on their cell doors and yell. I can guarantee its cathartic efficiency.

I wonder whether anyone will have the courage and imagination to transplant this play, with Joan Littlewood's Theatre Workshop production—excellent within the limitations, though there *must* be more of a break between night and dawn—to the West End. Aunt Edna and the matineé-goers might stay away but the Irish and the underworld would flock to it, to say nothing of us progressives.

* * *

iv. Waiting for the Hangman by *Richard Findlater**

In the South-West and East Ends, in Sloane Square and Angel Lane (E.15), new drama is booming—and without stars, too. This is a splendidly unnatural phenomenon in the English theatre, where audiences are notorious for blockading new talent, and I hope it will continue just as long as the subsidies to the Royal Court and Theatre Royal.

Down at the other Stratford (E.), Theatre Workshop is doing record business with the first play of an unknown author; and I have never felt this theatre, where so much brave and outstanding work has been done, so astir with the excitement that only a full house—and, it seems, capital punishment—can generate. For Brendan Behan's *The Quare Fellow* is set in a prison on the eve of a hanging, and abounds in clinical details of this judicial murder.

Revivals which have justly brought Theatre Workshop international fame have failed to lure more than a tiny handful of English playgoers: but everyone is interested in death, and a prime virtue of *The Quare Fellow* is the way it presents one of the facts of life usually avoided in the modern drama.

True, Mr. Behan's play is an indictment of capital punishment, and thus the Stratford box office benefits no doubt from the pathological zest with which a tiny minority of the public approaches anything to do with gallows. But *The Quare Fellow* is much more than an abolitionist play (as Ludovic Kennedy's *Murder Story* was, for example): It is good propaganda and good art. And, Mr. Behan being a poet, death is presented not only as an injustice but as a joke, for in the face of mortality his characters

* *Tribune* (London), (8 June 1956), p. 8.

show that gay and savage realism which gives so much of the Elizabethan drama its abiding power.

The impact of the play, of course, gains immeasurably from the fact that the author and most of the characters are volubly Irish. On the London stage, as every fugitive from Dublin knows, you can get away with murder in a brogue.

But *The Quare Fellow* could be almost as good a play if it was acted in Cockney, for its essential poetry is not something applied to the surface—a lacquer of blarney for beginners—but it springs from the situation and class of the characters.

The man condemned to death is never seen on the stage and Mr. Behan doesn't make the mistake of presenting his murderer as an obvious candidate for reprieve. The "quare fellow" waiting for the hangman butchered his brother in a highly unsympathetic fashion, for which no excuses are advanced, and for which no reprieve is possible.

What Mr. Behan emphasises, with the help of Joan Littlewood and her company (in what is probably the best directed *and* best acted production I have seen at Stratford) is the effect of the execution on the people in the jail—the warders, the chaplain, the other prisoners—as the grisly ritual nears its terrible climax.

With bitter, unsentimental realism the convicts discuss the chances of being slowly strangled; they fight to look at the condemned man's last meal; the warders, obliged to keep him company on his last night, show what compassion they can by leaving off their watches and shielding him from the sight of his grave; the visiting hangman, a jolly publican, borrows a warder's cap to look through the peep hole in the murderer's cell and judge the thickness of his neck; his last letters are thrown into the grave (so that they won't be sold to the Sunday papers); and the digging party (promised a Guinness each for their labours) pocket them in the hope of a profit.

Brendan Behan, an exuberant ex-member of the I.R.A., has spent eight of his thirty-three years in jail: he writes from experience. I am tempted to recommend a short course in Dartmoor or Brixton for some of our leading playmakers in the hope that it will teach them something about people—and, in particular, about non-U people who don't know they're being common when they reveal their emotions.

But perhaps it would be better to send Mr. Behan on short

courses to Belgravia, Surbiton, Gwaen-cae-gurwen, and other sections of English society. It would be a pity if he limited himself
to the Irish, about whom far too much has been written already.
For Mr. Behan is a born dramatist, with a rare talent for writing
about people, and hitherto his acquaintance with English people
has been arbitrarily limited by the police: he was forbidden to enter
this country from 1939 to 1952.

Now that he has, it seems, retired from politics, I hope he will
get down to writing plays. There are plenty of subjects left, even
when capital punishment is abolished.

* * *

v. Death's Jest Book by *Alex Matheson Cain**

To live in close contact with sudden, premeditated death, to
make it one's business—what effect does this have on a community
of men? This is the theme of a new play by Brendan Behan at the
Theatre Royal, Stratford, *The Quare Fellow*. The fellow himself,
whom we never meet, is in prison, and is going to be hanged; his
fellow-prisoners discuss him and hanging in general, the warders
suffer or take it in their stride, the hangman calculates the drop.
It is a roaring play, full of words and passion and fear, which seems
typically Irish.

Mr. Behan has spent eight years in various prisons for his I.R.A.
activities, and has spoken with men who have been condemned to
death. Those experiences he communicates here to us, enriched
with an extraordinary breadth of bawdy humour and tragic terror,
so that he avoids both human sentimentality and the problem-play
approach which one might expect from abolitionists. Judgment on
these questions is suspended, nor is there any psychological analysis
of motives. His prison is, indeed, a universe. The themes of the
play are the major ones of living and dying and suffering, and it is
surely not without design that analogies with the Crucifixion have
been introduced; besides specific references, there is the man
who has been reprieved just before the quare fellow was hanged,

* *The Tablet* (London), CCVII (9 June 1956), 540.

and there is the extraordinary final scene where the prisoners, digging the grave, gamble for the dead man's effects—his last letters—in order to sell them to the Sunday papers.

The scene of the hanging comes over as one of the most exciting and dynamic I have ever seen. First, a dead silence; then the tapping of messages on the water pipes—the prisoners' morse code—working up to a deafening climax to which is joined the clock chiming eight; the procession to the gallows is lunatically described in the style of a sports commentator over a megaphone; and then the noise of the drop. Passion could hardly have been strained further.

The play is excellently built up in contrasts of tension and comic relief, which is as crude and telling as the porter scene in *Macbeth*. Hanging, for these men, is a joke, because it is too close and terrifying to be taken seriously, and the bawdy ballad which comes out from behind the walls after the execution, and forms an accompaniment to the whole play, performs the same real function. Theatre Workshop has done a brilliant piece of work here.

* * *

vi. The Quare World of Brendan Behan by *Henry Hewes**

On the evidence of his American premiere, thirty-five-year-old Brendan Behan promises to be the most exciting new playwright to come out of Ireland since Sean O'Casey. His play *The Quare Fellow*, which has followed *The Iceman Cometh* into Circle-in-the-Square, is a rough-finished piece of work, but it never stops flaring up with the irrepressible flame of rebellion and subsiding into unforgettable afterglows in which the playwright captures the present moment in its poetic totality.

The play sets out with a series of descriptive scenes of what seems to be the normal routine of an Irish prison. But because Mr. Behan has spent eight of his thirty-five years in prison for I.R.A. activities the detail is supernormally rich. He finds an earthy humor in the prisoners' dodges, and particularly in those of two

* *Saturday Review* (New York), XLI (13 December 1958), 27–28.

elder convicts who manage to get drunk. While liquor is strictly forbidden, these two oldsters have found a way to manipulate regulations to their advantage. By going on sick call for rheumatism just before the official inspection, they oblige the guard to rub their legs with alcohol. And while he is occupied with his task they snatch swigs of the "methylated spirits". Then, Mr. Behan finds a social humor when he points out that a gentleman prisoner who has murdered his wife is accepted into the prisoners' fraternity, but that "a bloody sexual mechanic" is not. (He returns to this sort of humor later when a convict rises in outrage at a remark against the judiciary to defend the principle that "property must have security.") Finally, Mr. Behan finds a tragic irony in a reprieved prisoner's decision to hang himself rather than face eleven years of incarceration.

But the first act is merely prologue to a gathering storm which is to involve the deepest feelings of the inmates, the guards, and every one of us who actively or passively condones capital punishment. The title phrase, which is what the prisoners call a man to be hanged (significantly, they find it necessary to use a euphemism), applies to a character we never meet and know only through the comments of others. However, his quoted remark at sundown the night before his execution ("Aren't the evenings getting a grand stretch") commends him to us. And more important than the anxieties of a particular person's death are the anxieties evoked by society's deliberate execution of any man.

While there is a universal concern and guilt-stirring about the execution, each of the characters in the play expresses his own in widely varying ways. A cold-blooded stool-pigeon bets his Sunday allotment of bacon that the hanging will go through as scheduled. Another convict refuses to help prepare the grave despite the bonus of two cigarettes. The guards, too, become edgy, torn between officiousness and compassion. As one of them says, "This is a soft job between hangings." And even the hangman shows his deep-seated resentment of society for the inhuman job it has given him by his heavy drinking, his affected casualness, and his impersonal concentration on the mechanical details of the task ahead. If there is a central figure it is a guard named Regan, who has had a zealous religious upbringing and for whom each hanging constitutes a vicarious martyrdom.

Here is a good example of Mr. Behan's talent for drawing true characters rather than shallow personifications of a belief or attitude. It would have been much simpler to make Regan an enlightened opponent of capital punishment, but Mr. Behan has a knack for tapping the contradictions within human beings with each being a mixture of "good" and "bad", "right" and "wrong". While he seems to hold a Marxist view of the world ("What's a crook? Only a business man without a shop."), he is not doctrinaire about it. In his seemingly accurate dramatization of the twists and turns of intra-prisoner hostility and camaraderie he implies, without seeming to stack the cards, that it is more honest than the intra-guard relationships where they pretend friendliness but the very next second are betraying each other.

Mr. Behan's talent is undeniable, but he has also been most fortunate to have his play produced in the round at Circle-in-the-Square. Here, with a technique which has grown steadily from production to production over an eight-year period, Jose Quintero directs the action in such a way that we live on the character's level of existence. At the same time that he achieves this impression of naturalness he makes each portrayal into a full portrait, and gives the proceedings a shape and form by the way he moves his actors. Here he gets glorious assistance from his scenery: David Hay's simple but extremely effective construction of wooden ramps and a black wall on which has been painted in large letters "SILENCE". The first and last impression the audience receives is of that dead wall and the sound of a rebellious prisoner who defies its edict to sing the haunting "Along the Banks of the Royal Canal".

The performances are uniformly excellent. Most memorable perhaps are Lester Rawlins as the intense Regan; Liam Clancy as a cheeky young delinquent; Roy Poole as the prison bully; and Bryan Herbert and Barry Macollum as the two oldsters. The latter have an exchange on the advantage of prison life that is a play in itself. One says,

> We're too old and beat for lobbywatching and shaking down anywhere so that you'd fall down and sleep on the pavement of a winter's night and not know but you were lying snug and comfortable in the Shelburne.

And the other adds,

> Only then to wake up on some lobby and the hard floorboards under you and a lump of hard filth for your pillow, and the cold

and drink shaking you, wishing it was morning for the market pubs to open, where if you had the price of a drink you could sit in the warm anyway. Except, God look down on you, if it was Sunday.

Perhaps it is because these and the other actors perform with such refreshing truthfulness that we put ourselves in the frame of mind to soak in the poetic atmosphere of Mr. Behan's hard world. And though its special conditions may make it seem his world, not ours, we feel the same involvement in it that the play's characters feel in the special world of "the quare fellow".

6

Borstal Boy

i. Young Prisoners by *Maurice Richardson**

I can't think of anyone I would rather share a cell with than Brendan Behan in spite of the noise. Lively, generous, imaginative, and consistently cheerful, I would expect him to give out a sustained glow of euphoria like a sun-ray lamp of the emotions.

That is certainly what he does in this prison autobiography. Indeed there are moments when the flow of ideas and high spirits, the whole boisterous persona, tends to froth over and obscure slightly the larger view. In case this sounds like carping let me say now that *Borstal Boy* is an excellent book, vivid, solid, very warm and full of human observation, at least as good as Behan's admirers have the right to expect of him.

It opens with a bang in Liverpool in 1939: "Friday in the evening the landlady shouted up the stairs 'Oh God, oh Jesus, oh Sacred Heart, Boy, there's two gentlemen to see you.' " They were detectives come to arrest the sixteen-year-old Behan for explosive I.R.A. outrages for which he received a sentence of three years. After this and the preliminary interrogation, it divides up into Walton Gaol on remand, a Borstal reception centre, and finally an open Borstal in East Anglia.

The ugly things happen in Walton. There is one beastly affair, the slashing of a prisoner for taking another's cigarette-end. There follows the beating-up by prison officers (known as giving him a clean shirt!) of the slasher in his punishment cell, all the more sinister for happening off-stage.

The general climate is pretty tough. The language of course is frightful. Even in 1958 this book will burn a hole right through a maiden lady's shopping basket. Behan, for all his Celtic romanticism and Fenian mystique, is a most accurate transcriber of British

* The *Observer* (London), (19 October 1958), p. 21.

working-class dialects whether cockney or north country. He is not troubled by that strain of puritanism which, as he himself points out with sensitive sympathy, is an Irish social characteristic.

You do not expect a chronicle of prison life to read like Mrs. Gaskell, though Behan in his cell uses *Cranford* for one of those dramatic juxtapositions of which he is so fond. Another is his description of a priest taking Catholic prisoners and a scrimshanker or two round the Stations of the Cross. One of his strong points is his ability to mix this kind of heavy iron-gallows humour —as the Germans call it—with broad, cheerful clowning. His weakness is a tendency to lapse into stage Irish, both in style and thought. This seems to be due to an intermittent lack of discrimination which he needs to correct.

We do not get to the open Borstal until over halfway. This is where the surprise comes, for the rebellious Behan admits most freely that Borstal with its public school house and honour system is enjoyable—especially after Walton. He liked the staff and being well able to take care of himself got on with all his fellow prisoners, even the toughest. When one ran away he was quite upset to think of the governor being let down and had to correct himself with a start of Irish shame at "being sorry over anyone getting out of the clutches of the British Government". It is a pleasing tribute to the Borstal system that Behan should enjoy himself so much that his account of it, though hyper-realistic, diffuses an atmosphere of hilarious, almost Kiplingesque, adolescence. There are sharp sketches of fellow Borstalians in brilliantly characterised dialogue, but it is always Behan himself who is the centre of the stage.

* * *

ii. Rebel for a Cause by *Anon**

The name of a village in Kent has by now become synonymous with a system of training young offenders which, in spite of many

* The *Times Literary Supplement* (London), (24 October 1958), p. 606.

failures, has proved the most imaginative achievement of British penology. Based, perhaps too naïvely, on the traditions of the English public school, with its houses and captains and assumptions of "honour", Borstal became an easy target for the music-hall, though the spectacular increase in crime among boys and young men has of recent years made the jokes uncertain. And it may be that an optimism about the effect on young criminals of conditions of comparative freedom, with an emphasis on training rather than on punishment as such, has by this time been often sadly disappointed. Certainly—if statistics are a valuable guide—success, in terms of a subsequent law-abiding life, has latterly been less encouraging.

Mr. Behan, who was sentenced to Borstal training for I.R.A. activities during the war (he was too young for imprisonment), is not at all concerned with abstract considerations of penal reform. His book is a brilliantly evocative account of the effect of Borstal on a group of youths who bring to the enforced community life of such a place all their awkward individuations of upbringing and confirmed habits of violence and vice. They can seem to conform, and indeed they have their own loyalties and moments of generosity. But the impression is of a jungle that is only temporarily cleared, and at any moment the tigers will take over and the laws of the forest will be supreme.

Mr. Behan can afford to stand outside, for his offence, in his own conscience, has nothing in common with the dismal catalogue of grievous bodily harm and robbery and rape which are the credentials of his fellows. He is not at all censorious, but he exposes the rather pitiful helplessness of authority in the face of this troubled and treacherous world. And his stupendous gift of language, exuberant, ungoverned and indeed ungovernable, creates the very image of the rackety, reeking life of his wide boys, ponces, and screws.

But beneath the surface of this lewd and riotous book lies an essential charity which is altogether moving and memorable. Thus his picture of Charlie, the sailor who was his "china". (Mr. Behan's use of rhyming slang is throughout remarkable, and has for the first time given a literary stature to this acrobatic use of language.) Or, again, his deep understanding of Tom, the murderer of impeccable industry, the model prisoner who is essentially alone. These are more than the shrewd portraits, achieved by artifice, of the writer of imagination. They reflect, as does every page of the book, the capacity to see beyond the superficial level of bawdy talk and wicked deeds. Mr. Behan—and he will no doubt be surprised to hear it—in fact shares a quality which the best Borstal governors have: namely, a sense of justice that does not excuse, that is never surprised, and always remembers that, in the final analysis, society gets the crime it deserves.

Much in Mr. Behan's books is disturbing. Much of the picture he draws is a judgement on ourselves: on the values of a society which has created an army of psychopathic offenders which shows no signs of growing less. And the dilemma of Mr. Behan and of all other Irish rebels against English rule is clearly revealed, not least in the account of his difficulties with the priests who excommunicated him. But *Borstal Boy*, whatever one's judgement of crime or punishment or the ethics of rebellion, remains a work of unique authority in his confident evocation of the very breath and being of life under captivity. And scarcely ever can dialogue have been handled with such a virtuoso understanding of accent and rhythm, the very vocabulary of the world of the condemned.

* * *

iii. Out of Prison by *Peregrine Walker**

The flood of books from prison—cynical or sentimental, the crook's memoirs no less than the governor's—shows no sign of decrease, and by this time the mythology of screws and scarpering must be widely understood. But hardly a book has done more than satisfy curiosity at the superficial, and often sordid, level of anecdote and *reportage*. The effect of imprisonment on a man of sensibility and imagination has had to wait for the genius of Brendan Behan to record it.

Borstal Boy is a shocking book, which communicates the squalid, comic, seedy existence of a Borstal with alarming accuracy. For that reason it is not a book for refectory reading, though it is far from being obscene, if obscenity be defined in terms of the writer's in-

* *The Tablet* (London), (25 October 1958), 360–61.

tention. Mr. Behan, we can be sure, has taken the time he spent in Borstal as a uniquely compact episode for the writer's purpose, containing opportunities for seeing a group of boys and young men stripped of their defences: rebels against society who form now a society of their own, with its own loyalties and betrayals and its occasional moment of splendour.

Of course Mr. Behan was no ordinary Borstal Boy. Convicted, during the war, for I.R.A. activities, he was too young for the four-teen years prison sentence that would have been his fate had he been older, and he was sent to Borstal instead. He was in the proud tradition of Irish rebellion, and it is a strange concept of punish-ment that could suppose an English Borstal to be appropriate for such as he. He raises grave issues beneath the prodigality of his prose, and in particular his account of his excommunication makes uncomfortable reading. Whatever may have been true at the time of which he writes, it is certainly no longer the practice in English jails to exclude I.R.A. prisoners from the sacraments. And Mr. Behan's unsympathetic picture of the Catholic chaplain in the prison to which he first was sent—whom he names, and who has since died—leaves many questions unanswered.

Borstal Boy is notable on many counts—for its brilliant dia-logue, echoing so exactly the slang and the very intonations of young prisoners; for its memorably individual portraits, especially of Mr. Behan's own "chinas", with their fierce generosity; for its unconscious analysis of the psychology of the classic Irish rebel against English authority and assumptions. But it can only be recommended to the adult reader who can approach its Joycean coarseness and copiousness with detachment.

* * *

iv. Within the Gates by *Martin Sheridan**

Irish prison literature is a many-mansioned edifice—history has seen to that. Already, before *The Quare Fellow*, Brendan Behan had written sporadically of life under lock and key; but it was

* The *Irish Times* (Dublin), (25 October 1958), p. 6.

that amorphous *tour de force* which gained him entry to the citadel of which John Mitchel remains the most distinguished, though perhaps not the most amiable, occupant. With *Borstal Boy*, Mr. Behan, turned autobiographer, enhances his status within the gates.

The story opens when, at the height (as one gathers) of the bombing campaign in Britain, the author, a youthful I.R.A. emissary is picked up, together with a suitcaseful of gelignite, by the Liverpool police. What follows is the record of his progress through the machinery of British justice—police station, Bridewell and magistrate's court, remand prison assizes and the rest. The process takes more than 300 pages in the telling and two-thirds of it are over (the story is in three parts) by the time we get to Hollesley Bay, the "Open" Borstal Institution in East Anglia which gives the book its name.

In effect, *Borstal Boy* is a prison diary, but a diary with the dates —and little else—left out: a steaming *olla podrida* of a book into which the author seems to have cast practically everything that came to his hand. It says much for his skill as a storyteller that the narrative, in spite of its considerable weight of detail, moves briskly, except where, as happens all too often—about forty times by my reckoning—he clutters it with snatches of old songs. Mr. Behan is rightly proud of his pleasant tenor voice, of which Dublin audiences got a taste in *The Quare Fellow*, but enough is enough.

The nature of his material is another hurdle which, in my opinion, Mr. Behan has taken successfully. Present-day readers of fiction and biography are excessively familiar with the prison pattern—the boredom and cruelty, the stenches and lusts, the seedy jargon, the tribal taboos. *Borstal Boy* was all this and a great deal more. What makes it different is what distinguishes any piece of original writing—an individual style and a fresh approach:

> I was no country Paddy from the middle of the Bog of Allen to be frightened to death by a lot of Liverpool seldom-fed ——s, nor was I one of your wrap-the-green-flag-round-me junior Civil Servants that came into the I.R.A. from the Gaelic League, and well ready to die for their country any day of the week, purity in

their hearts, truth on their lips, for the glory of God and the honour of Ireland. No, be ———, I was from Russell Street, North Circular Road, Dublin, from the Northside.

(The blanks are mine. Mr. Behan used ball ammunition.)

This passage is significant as defining Mr. Behan's attitude to a number of things; the predicament which is his subject-matter, the nationalist tradition which put him there, and himself. Here, as elsewhere, he makes it clear that he has little time for the "Let Me Carry Your Cross for Ireland, Lord," school of patriotism. He professes unmitigated contempt for "bogmen", English as well as Irish—he met several of the former in Hollesley Bay: and he revels in his North Dublin ancestry and upbringing. Significantly, too, he discovers much common ground between his English fellow-inmates and himself:

> I had the same rearing as most of them, Dublin, Liverpool, Manchester, Glasgow, London. All our mothers had all done the pawn—pledging on Monday, releasing on Saturday. We all knew the chip shop and the picture house and the fourpenny rush of a Saturday afternoon, and the summer swimming in the canal and being chased along the railways by the cops.

Although he betrays no trace of regret for his I.R.A. activities Mr. Behan grew to like and respect his hosts:

> "Paddy, I think you like the bloody English."
> "Well, the English can love people without their being seven foot tall or a hundred years dead."

What made this growth of sympathy possible was his youth, which saved him from the "fourteenth stretch" which would certainly have been his if he had not been under eighteen at the time of his arrest. On remand in Walton Prison, a sort of cold hell which smelled and felt like a "refrigerated lavatory", he had learned, in spite of his defiance, to fear the English—at least, official England: the warders, mostly sadistic and foul-mouthed; the Governor, a George Arliss-headed old ———, "weary from his labours among the lesser breeds"; the chaplain (an Irishman once removed), who alienated him by trying to pressurise him into quitting the I.R.A. Mr. Behan cheeked the chaplain and was savagely beaten up. In Walton, too, he did a spell of Number-One-bread-and-water and solitary confinement—and listened to thuds and cries from the special punishment cells underground.

The contrast between Walton's rigour and gloom, and Hollesley, all sweetness and light, could hardly be more complete. Walton, for all its nineteenth-century nastiness, failed to take the shine off Mr. Behan—admittedly, it did not get much chance—and he started the final phase of his pilgrimage in excellent spirits after a Dickensian interlude in the Feltham allocation centre in London. Hollesley brought him the comparative freedom of the fields and the workshops, a troop of friends, and—very good for his ego, we gather—a "spot" in the annual concert as well as a first prize in the essay competition. In the end, when the sergeant who originally arrested him observes: "They've made a fine man of you, Brendan", Behan seems to concur. (It may be, indeed, if current London theatre criticisms can be relied on, that he got even more out of Hollesley than *Borstal Boy* suggests.)

In this book Mr. Behan has essayed, and I feel has succeeded in, a task in which a less exuberant, uninhibited and original talent might have failed. *Borstal Boy* is formless and uneven, and its characters are but lightly sketched. Scores, many of them grotesque, flash across its pages; few leave a lasting impression. What makes it succeed (for me) is the writing, which at its worst is fluent—with a capital F—and at its best is rich, ebullient, humorous and Rabelaisian. With Mr. Behan's droll asides, with his bursts of invective (an idiom that combines the Citizen and Private Carr), and with his many comic set-pieces, *Borstal Boy* is a very funny book, indeed. It derives additional piquancy from the author's habit of pulling the carpet from under people, himself not excluded. After a day on bread and water:

> if a warder came up and said, "Here you are, sing two lines of 'God Save the King' and I'll give you this piece of round steak," would I take it? Would I what? —— Mary and Joseph, he'd be a lucky man that I didn't take the hand and all off him.

It may be a paradoxical tribute to a book about prisons to say that it seldom afflicts the reader with the *rigor vitae* of the cell, but, Walton notwithstanding, this is not the least of *Borstal Boy*'s merits.

* * *

v. An Exuberant Irishman Adds to the World's Great Prison
Literature by *Gene Baro**

Brendan Behan was arrested in Liverpool in 1939, at the age of
sixteen; in his possession was found the kit of a bomb terrorist;
he had been working in England as a saboteur for the Irish Republican Army.

British public feeling was very much aroused against the Irish
Nationalist extremists, not only because of the deaths of innocent
men and women, but because of the aid and comfort to Nazi Germany that was implicit in the I.R.A.'s campaign of destruction and
demoralisation. Though British justice seemed sometimes unequal
to a moderate and dispassionate application of the law, yet, in
most cases, both the spirit and the letter of the law prevailed.
Brendan Behan was a juvenile offender; this memoir tells of his
arrest, imprisonment, trial, and remand to a Borstal Institution—
the British equivalent of the American reform school—and of his
life there and of the lives of his fellows in penal servitude.

Certainly, this book belongs with the world's great prison literature. Mr. Behan, who in recent years has become a fresh, strong
voice in the Anglo-Irish Theatre, gives us an exuberant narrative
of his years of incarceration. He brings alive the juvenile offender,
examines his self-regard, expounds his code, describes his tensions
and pleasures. We come to know these boys in feeling and in
thought; reading this book, we are caught up in a sense of immedi-
acy, as if we were overhearing these "judgments" of prison life, of
guards, governors, ecclesiasts, visitors, fellow convicts. We are in
the confidence of Behan and his mates, even as they were in the
confidence of one another; if we share in their rough, bawdy world
so close to violence, we recognise that it is also a world in which
fine human qualities can exist, loyalty, tenderness, charity.

Mr. Behan has recaptured the young voice of those bygone
years. This is no thoughtful, analytical retrospect, no armchair
appraisal of the past; the events of this story are discovered, so
to speak, in the living image of a sixteen-year-old Irish boy of
working-class parentage, a passionate fellow, brave, shrewd, sensitive, unsure. Tolerance pervades these pages, or perhaps it would
be fairer to say that these pages are marked by a growth of under-

* *New York Herald Tribune Book Review*, (22 February 1959), p. 5.

standing, by the very shaping of the narrator, and by his firm love of life. Here, for instance, is a prison memoir in which one is conscious of the turning seasons.

To be sure, there is some repetitiousness in this book, a number of loose ends, too; but its air of spontaneousness is its strength, and one does not miss a more formal organisation. Mr. Behan's prose has the vitality of good talk. It is racy, grounded in the particular, charged with feeling. The wit can be light or mordant. And Mr. Behan knows what to leave unsaid, often allowing his materials themselves to draw his moral for him. The prison slang, so inevitably a part of this book, heightens the sense of reality; a glossary of this special language is provided.

Altogether, *Borstal Boy* is memorable on many levels. Prison life is its chief ingredient, and the character and experiences of young Behan and his mates hold the imagination. But it also deals importantly through Behan—if perhaps unconsciously or incidentally—with the feelings of the I.R.A. men. And it is the story of a boy growing to manhood and to a firmer knowledge of himself, and it tells us most movingly of the mixture of good and evil in human kind.

* * *

vi. "To Show That Still She Lives" by *Frank O'Connor**

Brendan Behan, the author of *Borstal Boy*, was sent to England at the age of sixteen with supplies for Irish terrorists at work there and was arrested within forty-eight hours. As the British government was not legally in a position to hang a boy, he was sent for some years to an English reformatory for juvenile delinquents, where, clearly, he endeared himself to everybody.

This did not end his brushes with the law, British or Irish, and an Irish lawyer who represented him in one of his cases pleaded that the very sight of a policeman's uniform upset him. In his later years, he has become well-known as a dramatist without losing his fame as a limb of the devil.

During his first television interview he was very drunk, and British Broadcasting Corporation officials warned his interviewer,

* *Chicago Sunday Tribune*, (1 March 1959), p. 3.

Malcolm Muggeridge, that if Behan used his favourite four letter word, Muggeridge must not smile, but Behan was too drunk to utter any words. Yet he is one of the most popular men in Dublin.

Partly it is the Irish way of protesting against Ireland's new and terrible respectability, which resembles that of a lower class girls' college, "to show that still she lives", in the words of its national poet. But it is also because, in spite of his fist fights with policemen and his four letter words, Behan has never lost the sweetness that Irish people love. Dublin is full of stories of his kindness to old people, sick people, and down and outs.

It is important to remember this when you read *Borstal Boy* or you will get an entirely false impression of the book. The Irish "nervous Nellies" have banned it as "indecent", but Catholic papers in England have enthused about it, and any thoughtful reader will soon see why.

At the age of sixteen, which, in Ireland, is equivalent to an American twelve, Behan was beaten by a policeman and by sadistic warders at the instigation of a beastly Irish priest, and he describes these things with a swagger and obscenity that is sometimes shocking.

But when you cease to notice the four letter words you become aware that behind them is a shuddering sensibility and the innocence of an acolyte, and at the end you are left with an impression that is—there is no other word for it, tho' I shall probably need brass knuckles to defend me against Behan for having mentioned it—edifying and inspiring.

If I am a little unhappy about the book, it is not because I think it can do anything but good, but because Behan is not the only young Irish writer who has been forced into violent exhibitions of nonconformity, and I am afraid that his mannerisms may grow on him and overlay the quality in him that makes *Borstal Boy* important.

* * *

vii. Borstal Revisited by *Corey Phelps**

Brendan Behan is remembered both for his work, the plays *The Quare Fellow* (1954) and *The Hostage* (1958) and his autobiographical novel *Borstal Boy* (1958), and for his frenetic public life (1956–64), chronicled in the daily press and on national television—remembered perhaps more for the vitality of both than the substance of either. He died creatively sometime in 1959–60, cause uncertain, and physically in 1964, of alcohol, diabetes, jaundice and pneumonia—at the age of forty-one.

Of the ten books that appeared under his name, only with *Borstal Boy* did Behan overtly participate in preparing the manuscript for publication,[1] editing, re-writing, correcting proofs, forcefully imposing himself (though possibly, in the end, not forcefully enough). By the time of publication he had re-written nearly the entire book twice and parts of it three and four times. He had an abiding affection for the plays, but those who knew him said there was a special attachment to *Borstal Boy*, that he considered it his finest achievement.[2]

Three manuscripts in the Special Collections of Morris Library notes for and extracts from his early work on *Borstal Boy*, offer unique insights into the evolution of the book—and of Brendan Behan as an author. The manuscripts are the first lines and images on a new canvas, a canvas which would be painted over many times on the way to completion.

Born into a family pervaded with fervent support of Irish nationalism, Behan was to spend most of his early manhood (sixteen to twenty-three) incarcerated for politically-related offences—offences whose prime motivation, his biographers have pointed out,[3] was probably more a need for personal recognition than pure nationalistic fervour.

In December 1939, eight years after joining the junior movement of the Irish Republican Army, sixteen-year-old Behan entered Liverpool with a suitcase containing incendiary devices. Though it was at the time of the I.R.A.'s bombing campaign in Britain, this

* *1 Carb S* (Southern Illinois University Library), II (Winter–Spring 1975), 39–60.

was in all likelihood an independent undertaking. He was arrested almost upon arrival, held in Walton Jail, and sentenced to three years' Borstal (reform school) detention. Given an early release late in 1941 and deported to Dublin, Behan was not long getting into further trouble—at Easter 1942 he was arrested for trying to murder two policemen. During an incident between Special Branch detectives and some I.R.A. men, Behan had grabbed a revolver and fired several rounds at the police. (He missed.) As with the Liverpool incident it was more an expression of personal bravado than a revolutionary act. This time he was given sentences totalling fourteen years and sent, initially, to Dublin's Mountjoy Prison.

Behan would use his circumstances to good advantage. The experiences would form the basis for his two finest works, *Borstal Boy* and *The Quare Fellow*, and in Mountjoy (and later in the Curragh Camp) he would begin to work seriously as a writer.

He had first been published when he was twelve, the year before his formal education ended. In the late 1930s he had contributed poems and articles to Republican journals. Now, starting four years' imprisonment (he would be released in the general political amnesty of 1946), he began to write almost immediately. Sean Kavanagh, then Governor of Mountjoy, encouraged Behan greatly, providing special facilities for his writing and arranging for Sean O'Faolain to visit the young author in prison and read some of his work;[4] this in turn lead to further encouragement from O'Faolain, publication and pay. He would compose a substantial body of work: a full-length play (*The Landlady*, which he also translated into Irish), the first version of *The Quare Fellow*, and scores of short stories, sketches and articles. Among the latter were several pieces on his recently completed Borstal days. One of them was published—his first paid work—in the June 1942 issue of *The Bell*, and in December 1943 he mentioned more of his work on this theme, a short story called "Borstal Day" and some pieces about the 1939 bombing campaign.[5]

Another article from this time was titled "The Courteous Borstal", the autograph manuscript of which is in Morris Library. It is a short piece, twelve pages with many cross-outs and corrections, and in it Behan gives a rather cursory accounting of the period between his arrest in Liverpool and his removal to Hollesley Bay Borstal. It seems more an attempt to get ideas and remembrances down on paper (where they could later be expanded) than it does a finished piece. As such, "The Courteous Borstal" could represent Behan's preliminary notes for the first half of *Borstal Boy*.

A fellow political prisoner recalls sitting in Behan's cell at this time and watching him work, "furiously, writing page after page, letting them flutter to the floor."[6] (Behan showed some of his work to the other prisoner and asked him to comment, but the other man couldn't decipher the script very well.) "The Courteous Borstal" appears to have been written hastily, the penmanship gradually disintegrating as it tried to keep up with the author's thoughts. It looks as though he stopped in the middle of page eleven, then went back to it later in a more leisurely mood. (This was the only period in which Behan wrote in longhand, subsequently using a typewriter almost exclusively.)

Behan begins the piece with a reflection on his acceptance at Hollesley Bay Borstal—an acceptance by his peers and the administration that, inasmuch as it influenced his attitudes towards Englishmen (allowing him to differentiate between the citizens on the one hand, and their country's Irish policy on the other), was to become a major theme of the book.

> If we'd had girls in Hollesley Bay I'd have applied to spend the rest of my life there[.] Nowhere else have I met an almost classless society. Nowhere was I loved so well, or respected so highly. I've my letters home to prove that I thought that at that time, too, I loved Borstal boys and they loved me. (Manuscript page 1.)

This theme, in the book, would more be illustrated than stated outright, and would be balanced by occasional exceptions. By the nature of his crime (attempted terrorist bombing in an England at war) Behan was fortunate to have been treated with civility, let alone loved and respected—as Behan was well aware. That he *was* accepted as an individual (rather than as an extension of what he seemed to represent) allowed him to consider his jailers and fellow inmates in the same light. It was a major contribution to his growth as a young man, which he duly recorded in *Borstal Boy*.

A theme that was not to be expanded in the finished book, however, was homosexuality in Borstal. "The Courteous Borstal", in fact, contains Behan's clearest and most straight-forward statement on that aspect. Conditions at Hollesley Bay were agreeable,

But the absence of girls made it that much imperfect. Homosexuality (of our sort) is not a substitute for ~~ordinary~~ normal sex. It's a different thing, rather similar to that of which T. E. Lawrence writes in ["] The Seven Pillars." (p. 1)

Further on in the manuscript, Behan distinguishes between the "youth of healthy muscle and slim wrought form" and the "powdered pansy[,] who feels himself a contradiction of his physical equipment", adding that the latter has every right to be that, or anything else he wants to be.

Our lads saw themselves beautiful and had to do something about it. About ~~two~~ a third[s] of them did. Another third, not so influential or less good looking would have liked to. However[,] without women it could not be a pattern of life, only a prolonging of adolescence – it was as beautiful as that. (pp. 2–3)

It is a candid statement, made with simplicity, sincerity and innocence. References to this element of Borstal life in the finished book—the incident involving Charlie and Shaggy (p. 279),[7] and the relationship between Shaggy and Leslie—would be treated with sensitivity, but would also be much more guarded and vague. In "The Courteous Borstal", homosexuality is an important and positive experience; in *Borstal Boy* it is of little moment, and the connotation is negative.

The manuscript further provides excellent examples of Behan revising his work, searching for the right words and the best order in which to use them. Defining what he meant by "powdered pansy", he wrote:

who ~~feels himself~~ ~~equi wrongl~~ ~~equipped~~
~~mentall~~ y
~~with physical~~ feels himself a contradiction
of his physical equipment. (p. 2)

The thought process would have been something like this:

who feels himself equi[pped] . . .
who feels himself wrongly equipped . . .
who feels himself mentally equipped with physical . . .
who feels himself a contradiction of his physical equipment.

The general impression, years later, would be that words fell from Brendan Behan simply and without exertion, that he'd only to open his mouth and out poured a *Quare Fellow* or a *Borstal Boy*. To an extent Behan himself encouraged that myth. But it never was true; he worked with the words till he had what he wanted, and it was hard work, creating a finished product that would *seem* effortless.

Behan touches on a number of additional elements that would later be expanded, either specifically or in kind, in the book: the interview with the Lady Visitor at Feltham; the descriptions of the various Borstal Institutions and the kinds of boys that were selected for each; the friendly "screw" with whom he discussed the wiring of mines, and who provided him extra potatoes. He glosses over his physical and mental pain at Walton Jail, where he was held awaiting trial. He mentions "insulting by brutal behaviour of the Roman Catholic chaplain and the prison doctor", and comments that the warders were worse than swine, but goes into no detail. There is a note in the margin, "a chronicle of torture", but it is crossed through and he lets the matter drop with "That is as much as I want to say of my pre-Borstal captivity" (p. 4). The piece ends with the boys chained together, on their way to Borstal in chara-bancs. "I'm sure the people on the road took us for holidaymakers, for every conceivable song was sung on the ninety miles from Felt-ham to Hollesley Bay" (p. 12). It is the kind of juxtaposition—chained prisoners/singing holidaymakers, the human capacity to rise above circumstance—that would make *Borstal Boy* affecting.

In 1960, asked about his prison writing, Behan dismissed it with: "Anything written in jail is rubbish, and that includes *Pilgrim's Progress*."[8] Precious little of his work at Mountjoy and the Curragh Camp has survived, yet "The Courteous Borstal", while not up to the quality or technique of the work he was doing even a few years later, is not rubbish. It hints of talent throughout, and here and there reveals that talent. One has the impression that in 1960 Behan was more concerned with providing a quote for the *New York Times* than with giving an honest appraisal of his work from his jail period.

Completing his last major imprisonment in 1946 (there would later be brief periods in jail for breaking the English deportation order, and for fighting and drunkenness), Behan wrote more articles and stories, a new one-act play, and a dozen or so poems in Irish in the late 1940s. From 1951 onward he made more and more of his living as a writer: free-lance journalism in Dublin, later a regular column for one of the papers, scripts for Radio Eireann, occasional magazine pieces. *The Quare Fellow* was presented in Dublin (1954) and in London (1956), the latter production allowing him to give up journalism for the most part and concentrate on writing another play and on finishing *Borstal Boy*.

He had envisioned a book on his Borstal days almost from the beginning. In a letter of December 1943, he wrote that his experiences in England "provided me with material for a book on Borstal which I'll get fixed up after the war and with material for numberless short stories."[9] He had already started "a long novel" on the 1939 bombing campaign, "title 'The Green Invader',"[10] which he would later combine with the Borstal theme.[11] (Behan frequently referred to this book as a novel, though it was later billed as an autobiography. It is a bit of both. What matter if the boy playing St. Joseph in the Nativity play was "in" for non-attendance at school?[12] It made a better story if he'd pushed his crippled brother over a cliff to his death.[13] As Dominic Behan observed of his brother's storytelling, "there was a general truth about Brendan's account of everything—and much more entertaining."[14])

In the early 1950s extracts from his work would begin to be published—"Bridewell Revisited" in the Paris-based *Points* (1951), a series of six articles in Irish in *Comhar* (1952–53). (These two magazines gave Behan considerable encouragement at the time he was trying to establish himself as a writer. *Comhar* subsidised a stay in Aran to improve his Irish as an advance against a book in that language on his I.R.A. and prison remembrances, but Behan spent more time teaching the Aran men his Dublin idioms than vice versa and the book did not materialise—in Irish.[15]) In 1956 Borstal extracts were serialised in the Irish edition of the *Sunday Dispatch*.

It was a golden time for Behan, writing *Borstal Boy*. He would be at his typewriter by seven in the morning, writing a page or two, perhaps picking up a book or going out for a walk to marshal his thoughts, then returning to his typewriter and more work.[16] Generally he would write till noon, then take the rest of the day for himself. He was drinking almost nothing and adhering (diabetes had been diagnosed) to a strict diet: a Behan ordered, disciplined, work-oriented—productive.

In the winter of 1956–57 the editorial director of the London publishing firm, Hutchinson, went to Dublin and gave Behan a generous advance on the Borstal book; early in June Behan delivered a 300-page typescript, promising a final instalment of 100 pages in the near future.[17] In August he went with his wife to Connemara, where he wrote the final chapters, posting them to Hutchinson on September 20.[18]

Behan was painstaking with *Borstal Boy*, re-writing, editing, refusing to part with the manuscript until he was satisfied with it. By the time he had corrected the proofs it was substantially modified from the initial conception.[19] Two typescripts in Morris Library, extracts from his early production on the book, provide unique intelligence on these changes—especially rare in that all but a few pages of his early drafts were destroyed. Beatrice Behan, for example, had entered their cottage in Connemara on the September day her husband typed the last page of his final version to find him tearing manuscript pages in half and burning them in the fireplace, explaining that he was "tidying up" before they returned to Dublin. She recognised the pages as being from an early draft of the book and asked why he was destroying them. "I don't want people reading my notes when I'm dead," he answered. She managed to save a few of the pages by grabbing them from him and running away. But very few.[20]

The typescripts were acquired by Morris Library in the late 1960s amongst the archives of Dublin's *Envoy* magazine (1949–51). Neither were published in that journal. The poetry editor of *Envoy* was Valentin Iremonger. It was Iremonger (possibly from his knowledge of the typescripts in *Envoy*'s files) who had brought *Borstal Boy* to the attention of Hutchinson's editorial director, Iain Hamilton. In fact, when Hamilton went to Dublin to meet Behan and read his work, it was specifically on Iremonger's advice.[21] Hamilton was "so impressed with the thirty-odd pages of typed foolscap that he . . . signed Brendan up on the spot", for an advance of £350.[22] This raises the fascinating possibility that the thirty pages now in Morris Library are the basis on which Hutchinson purchased *Borstal Boy*—if not the actual pages, then possibly the original typescripts from which later copies were typed.

The longer of the two typescripts (twenty pages of text) is titled

"Bridewell Revisited". A note in Behan's hand on the un-numbered title page reads, "A bit that I am not ashamed of—the title supplied by John Ryan [editor of *Envoy*] for whom my affection is tenacious, invincible and reckless." (Behan was so fond of the title that he used it again five years later for another extract from his Borstal work, concerning the Nativity play, published in the *New Statesman*.[23])

"Bridewell Revisited" tells the story of Behan's arrest in Liverpool, his incarceration in Dale Street Bridewell, and his early friendship with the cockney sailer, Charlie. An early version of the first twenty pages of the eventual book, it appeared in the winter 1951–52 number of *Points*, a little magazine published in Paris by Sinbad Vail, an American. The piece was edited for publication, probably by Vail. Most of the passages cut for the magazine were put back in for the book, though usually in a revised form. Behan sent the "Bridewell" typescript to Vail in May 1951, commenting that "Some months ago, I wrote you that I had started a book. I am calling it *Borstal Boy*. Here is a bit of it."[24] He wrote Vail again in June, referring to the typescript: "You must excuse the terrible typing. It was not my fault. I had to do it myself. No typist in Dublin would look at it."[25]

A primary difference between the typescript version and the book edition is of tone: the typescript reads as if it were written by a youngster (passionate, awkward, raw-talented) living the events, while the corresponding section of the book contains an edge of maturity, an adult looking back on his youth. Professor Boyle's point is well taken that the typescript possesses a mood of "immaturity, irresponsibility, and foolish adolescence" which "fits both the truth of Behan's character and the thematic requirements of his book", and that the book section "seems somehow short of the mark. . . ."[26] The point is not that the final version is spurious or poorly written—it is neither—but rather that the earlier version is in some ways superior.

This change in tone is evidenced, primarily through changes of phrasing and rhythm, in scores of small alterations made throughout the text:

> "How old are you, Paddy?" asked the sergeant.
> "Sixteen, seventeen in February." (Ts. p. 3)

> "I'm sixteen, and I'll be seventeen in February." (*Borstal Boy* p. 4)

"Like that song, Pad?"
"Smashing, china."
Speak it like a native. English in three days[.] (Ts. p. 17)

> "Smashing, china." I speak it like a native, English, in two days
> and a bit. (*Borstal Boy* p. 17)

A major change in the same vein is more injurious in its effect on
the text. Following his arrest in Liverpool, Behan was taken to
C.I.D. headquarters. He refused to answer any questions, but:

> I agreed to make a statement, with a view to propaganda, for the
> Republic. Ultimately, I suppose, for myself. Revolutionary politics
> are forms of acting. Ghandi ne'er cast a clout, nor Goering ne'er
> turned a jowl camerawards with more care than I took with that
> statement.
>
> "My name is Brendan Behan. I came over here to fight for the
> Irish Worker's and small Farmers republic, for a full and free life
> for my fellow countrymen, north and south, and for the removal
> of the baneful influence of British imperialism from Irish affairs.
> God save Ireland."
>
> The God save Ireland was an extra bit of hypocrisy, intended
> for the Dublin papers, for the people at home who would be
> reading them. (Ts. p. 5)

The same incident, in the book, is considerably revised.

> I agreed to make a statement, with a view to propaganda for the
> cause. It would look well at home, too. I often read speeches from
> the dock, and thought the better of the brave and defiant men
> that made them so far from friends or dear ones.
>
> [The statement is made virtually unchanged. It is followed by
> one of the policemen observing that the only farmers in his experi-
> ence have been "bloody big fellows"; and by Behan commenting
> on how his statement will be received within the Republican
> movement.]
>
> The "God Save Ireland" bit made me feel like the Manchester
> Martyrs, hanged amidst the exulting cheers of fifty thousand fair-
> play merchants, and crying out with their last breath:
>
> [Song]   (*Borstal Boy* pp. 6–7).

The original is concise, candid and fresh—the revised version, by
comparison, clumsy and cluttered. Most dearly regretted of course
is the loss of Behan's candour and insight regarding revolutionary
politics, the nicely turned comparison of the public relations and
theatrical aspects of his statement, Ghandi's clout, and Goering's

jowl. Simply, it is Behan at the top of his form: wise, shocking, funny, terse, and unexpected. The Manchester Martyrs, a bit of a song, and humorous comments on the physical stature of farmers are all well and good, but they blur the moment and make it flabby.

Another cut typescript passage (one of the few to be cut in both the magazine and book versions) raises the possibility of censorship. The Bridewell turnkey has brought Behan dinner ("Three dirty potatoes on an enamel plate, two slices of dry bread and a mug of water"), and takes the opportunity to assault the prisoner verbally. He says the Irish, inside a pub on Saturday night, are good soldiers—but that after a few hours in jail they crack up. "What will you be like after twenty years, Paddy? That's if you're lucky and they don't ang you." The jailer continues that the food is good enough for the prisoner, that it's better than what he got at home, and adds that Behan will be living on less before he gets out.

Behan, in his own mind, invokes the names of Irishmen who died fighting the fascists in Spain, apologizing to them for what he is about to say:

> Tommy Woods, Mick May, Jack Nulty, Dinny Coady, Tony Fox. The young, ragged, dead at Albacete, Brunete, Gaudalarja [sic], Harama, on University Hill and on the Ebro. Forgive me. A scalded heart will say many is the thing.

The turnkey persists, calling Behan a "treacherous Irish bastard. I ope they ang you as igh as Nelson." But Behan, wounded, takes no more. He spits out that the Germans won't be long in knocking Nelson down, nor the entire town; that they will "leave Liverpool a heap of cinders", and the turnkey buried under the rubble of the Bridewell.

> He pushed me into the cell and banged ou[t] the door. I stood looking at the plate and mug on the bench.
>
> I thought of Ernst Toller and of the demonstration I marched in when I was twelve, because they would not let him enter Ireland. And I allowed that stupid old swine of a turnkey to rile me into betraying myself. Into applauding Tollers jailers, the murderers, the killers of his swallows.[27]
>
> I walked up and down the cell for a while[,] looked at the plate of potatoes and bread, sat down and ate most of it. (Ts. pp. 18–19)

It is a fine piece of craftsmanship. Outwardly he gets the best of the jailer, or at least "gives as good as he got". But he is well aware that he got the *worst* of himself as well, that he denied his beliefs in a fit of temper; and it is because of this knowledge that he paces his cell.

As is the case with most of the altered sections of the book, the corresponding part of *Borstal Boy* (p. 19) is not, of itself, weak; only when compared to the original does it seem flaccid. The turn-key delivers the same meal (except that the potatoes are now half-rotten as well as dirty), and makes basically the same ethnic and national slurs, after which he merely closes the door and leaves. Behan again paces his cell, but this is now motivated by his revulsion at the food and because of the numbing cold weather. The original is perceptive and reveals a great deal about the character and the times in which he lived; the revised version tells us only that he found the ambience and cuisine at Dale Street Bridewell wanting.

How much did censorship, self-imposed or otherwise, have to do with the excising of the bombing remarks? The passage could certainly have proven offensive to English sensibilities in the 1950s. Not only had Liverpool indeed been severely bombed in the war, but for the remarks (no matter how eloquent the accompanying disclaimer) to come from one with I.R.A. affiliations could prove especially repugnant. One element within the Irish Republican movement had been pro-Nazi, more from hatred of Britain than any affection for Germany. Behan was not of this element, having been anti-fascist in his public actions and in his writing since his early teens. (At fifteen he had lied about his age and volunteered to fight on the Republican side in the Spanish Civil War. But his mother intercepted his acceptance notice, and he did not go to Spain.) Perhaps it was felt that this distinction, especially in light of Behan's connection with the 1939 bombing campaign, would not be made. The passage in the typescript simply is too good—far superior to the corresponding book section—to have been cut for no reason.

Behan wrote that in *Borstal Boy* he had tried "to reproduce the conversations of adolescent prisoners about sex and religion and sometimes about politics and sometimes about crime and sport."[28]

Compulsive profanity, an elemental part of the original dialogue, was heavily censored; and the results were damaging.

The profanity is indigenous to the truth both of Behan's characters and their circumstances. Four-letter words occupy nearly every paragraph of the "Bridewell" typescript, but their effect, because of the way Behan uses them, is not offensive. Any shock value is quickly eliminated through reiteration ("like the barrack-room drone before lights out in which repetition so saps emphasis that the words take on the hypnotic power of a litany"[29]), after which the words become an important element of Behan's prime strength as a writer: the ability to write dialogue with a pulse and tone that are authentic, and, at the same time, poetic.

Neither *Points* nor Hutchinson would print the original language. Vail balked at it almost immediately, asking Behan to make alterations. But Behan had sent Vail his only copy of the "Bridewell" typescript, and wrote him in June 1951, "I wonder would it be a terrible big thing to ask you to do whatever excising you would think necessary? For the . . . and so forth, could you manage an initial and a dash? It *is* an extract from a novel. Why shouldn't it read like that?"[30] (Most of the alterations in the typescript are in a hand other than Behan's—in light of the foregoing, probably Vail's.) Hutchinson combined initial-and-dash substitution with deliberate misspelling ("fugh", "facquing").

These alterations not only damage the authenticity and rhythm of the dialogue, but their application implies that the original was obscene (otherwise, why change it?)—which was neither Behan's intention nor, as witnessed by the "Bridewell" typescript, his result. (It is instructive that the word is used as an adjective, an adverb, a noun and a pronoun—but rarely as a verb, and never in the sense of sexual intercourse.) Finally, to call attention to the profanity by dashes and misspellings is to give it undue weight—to make it a Prussian blue slash on a canvas of oranges and browns, when in fact it is an ochre: blending, inconspicuous.

Hutchinson's decision to censor the language was criticised at the time of the book's publication by a columnist in the *Spectator* (though acknowledging that Hutchinson allowed Behan greater latitude than he was likely to find elsewhere).[31] Robert Lusty, then chairman of the Hutchinson Publishing Group, responded. Stating that the decision to alter had been made by himself, he agreed that the rhythm of Behan's dialogue was a major element of his style, and that "the missing word" makes an important contribution to the rhythm. But he argued that "dialogue is for speech and the constant repetition of the word in the cold formality of type detracts from this rhythm and accentuates only its typographical ugliness";[32] in other words, that something going to the mind by way of the eye is more emphatic than something going by way of the ear. (The reverse is arguable.) Lusty continued that "the fear that the book might be driven under the counter" also affected his decision, although maintaining that "fear of legal repercussions" was not a consideration.

It is not difficult to appreciate sympathetically their various motivations: Behan, struggling to establish himself, proud of his work, eager to have it published; Vail and Hutchinson eager to avoid controversy, legal or otherwise; all certainly eager to reach the widest possible audience. And yet the fact remains that, to the detriment of the work, the language was censored; and the final irony that a small expatriate, *avant garde*, literary magazine and the very big firm, Hutchinson of London, chose to deal with the issue in much the same manner.

The shorter typescript, titled "From 'Borstal Boy', a work in progress by Brendan Behan", is in two parts—the first of which (five pages) concerns Callan, another Irish prisoner at Walton Jail. It apparently was never published until, in revised form, it appeared in the book (see especially pages 130–31).

Set on the eve of the executions of two I.R.A. men (elsewhere in England), the extract tells the story of Callan's rebellious and noisy defiance of his jailers, and of Behan's attempts at avoiding involvement.

Two months in Walton Jail have left Behan "very anxious for a truce with the British. I'd have given them another six counties to be left alone" (Part 1: page 1); and he tries to spend a quiet evening in bed, reading a novel, hoping Callan ("a mad Republican," in jail for stealing an overcoat) will cause no trouble over the executions. But Callan, in the cell beneath Behan's, does not cooperate:

"Uuuuup the Republic!"
He let a roar out of him would wake Robert Emmet.
"Aaaah you bastaaards!"

A roar that would put him back in his box.
"Good oul Hiiiiteler, thats the boy for you bastaaaaards!"
"Jesus, they'll kill us all", I shivered to myself in bed. (1: 2)

Callan calls out Behan's name, and, torn between his own Republicanism and concern for his physical well-being, Behan goes to the ventilator in his cell.

"Go soirbhighid Eire", I whispered, down the ventilator, softly so as the screws wouldn't hear me, and in Irish so as they wouldn't understand me if they did.
"I can only hear a little whisper", roared Callan.
"Im shouting at the top of my voice", I whispered back, "the walls here are three feet thick". (1: 3)

Callan (who doesn't understand Irish) continues his roaring. Realising that more would be expected of himself, "a soldier-like symbol of the living Republic", Behan continues to whisper responses down the ventilator in Irish, when he hears Callan's door being opened.

Kick—grunt. Baton on head—squeal. Punch in mouth—moan. Knee in crotch—squeal. Further knees in crotch—moan. Knee in crotch and batons in kidneys—moan and whine and moan. (1: 4)

Apprehensive of being later criticised for his timidity, Behan decides to keep at his whispers till Callan loses consciousness. A "screw" appears at his own door and demands to know what he's doing at the ventilator. "I'm saying my prayers, sir." The jailer grumbles, but goes away, and, Behan continues his novel until lights out.

The extract was tightened for inclusion in the book. The use of Irish was discarded, as well as the sounds of Callan's beating, and the concern that Callan might criticise his lack of enthusiasm. (The reference to Hitler also was cut.) The alterations do not have a large effect on the book one way or the other, although they do combine to give the scene less dimension, and a somewhat muted urgency.

On the fourth page of "The Courteous Borstal", Behan started to write about maltreatment by officials at Walton Jail. As mentioned earlier, he put a note in the margin, "a chronicle of torture", but then crossed out the note and dropped the subject. "A

Chronicle of Torture" would make an apt title for the second part (four pages) of the shorter typescript—torture of the spirit.

His time at Walton is almost over. Soon he will be sent to Feltham Boys Prison (the Borstal allocation centre), where "you could talk, eat plenty, wear pyjamas and sleep in a dormitory. Where the screws wore no uniforms and kept their batons in their trousers pockets" (2:1). It will, for Behan, mean deliverance from the human wreckage administering Walton Jail: deliverance from the warders who punish the boys for whispering at exercise, from the prison Governor, "A dying wizened old corpse, maimed by God that Man might mark him, curse him, shun him, except in a prison where the Marquis de Sade is Head Buck Cat" (2:1).

In a bitter stream of anger and hatred, Behan speaks of deliverance from the Chief Warder,

> "Good type this Hunt, stern disciplinarian, dont know how wed get on without him["]. Make a splendid—railway detective, labour spy, night-watchman, game-keeper, bank messenger. "Half a crown for your trouble, my man". "Thank you sir, glad to be of service, sir". Black and Tan, Palestine Policeman, clean as a whistle [. . .] faithful employee. "Robert, when you take over, remember Hunt. He's given very loyal service. Particularly good at weeding out undesirable types. Remember him, let not poor Hunty starve". Prison service, good opening for right man, Chief Warder, Chief Bully of the wretched, the broken, the young. (2:2)

It will mean deliverance from the doctor who prescribes mechanical restraint, from the priest who proclaims charity and God's love and sends a boy before the Governor for talking at service, from the parson who makes sexual advances at the boys, from the Principal Officer, who enjoys

> . . . the burnings of the sweepings after haircutting—with an appreciative grin—"Can yer ear the nits crackin', Paddy?" [He wasn't as bad as some of the others, but:] He didn't have to be; his pension well earned and his service nearly over. After thirty years of spying, bullying and torturing, he relaxes . . . jests.
> "Can yer 'ear the nits crackin, Paddy?"
> Nunc Dimmitus. . . . (2:4)

Stylistically this is a Brendan Behan we rarely meet in the later work, but is much evidenced in his other writing from this time—the poems (in the good translations) and short fiction, and the second version of *The Quare Fellow*. When expressing **extreme** emotion Behan would sometimes use a swelling stream of words— as if, in effect, it had all welled up inside him and burst forth of its own volition, that he could not stop it, that it would run its own course and finish only when it had spent itself. The piece was not included in the book, nor published elsewhere.

The decision to censor the language was not Behan's, but he agreed to it readily (at least with Vail). It is an area of which we know the decisions and their effects, the people who made them and the motivations involved. The general editing done on the book, however, is much more obscure and difficult to comprehend.

It is not a question of the text being corrupted. Some of the alterations improve the final product (for instance, in the "Bride-well" typescript Charlie, the cockney sailor, had deserted the navy and was arrested for "a desperate random burglary to get civilian clothes" (p. 11). This was in conflict with Charlie's later character development—his pride in being a sailor—and was rightly cut). And, finally, we do not know all the specifics of Behan's participation and cooperations in the final editing of the manuscript.

Certainly Behan was vitally interested in the editing of his material. When Iain Hamilton went to Dublin and bought the rights to the book, Behan had become angry when Hamilton wanted to take the unfinished manuscript back to London. "You'll get no fucking book until I'm finished with it," he told him.[33] Indeed, Behan later was reluctant to part even with his 300-page type-script; the publishers had practically to coerce the pages from the author, and next morning he was in their offices, demanding return of his typescript, claiming it wasn't finished. Hamilton suggested that Behan go back to Dublin and finish the book while editing started on the 300 pages. Behan replied that an author was the best judge of his work's suitability for publication, his eyes searching the room for the typescript. But the pages had, as a precaution, been locked in a drawer, and Behan was eventually persuaded to leave without them.[34]

The editing process for *Borstal Boy* was a long one. More than a year passed between receipt of the bulk of the manuscript and Behan's correction of the proofs. We do not know if the balance of the book was altered as extensively as the first twenty pages.

Not only did Behan burn his early drafts, but all but a few pages
of the manuscript (and only copy) of the final pre-edited version
were, at his request, destroyed as well.[35] He was asked about the
amount of re-writing that went into his books and plays. "Ah, an
ocean of new words . . . but despite what you read, I do it myself,
naturally with the help of editors and directors. And what's wrong
with that? And where would Tom Wolfe have been without Max
Perkins, also James Jones?"[36] While it seems unlikely that Behan
would, of his own volition, have cut some of the passages pre-
served in the typescripts in Morris Library, there is little doubt
that he was satisfied both with the process and with the result.

The spring following publication of "Bridewell Revisited" Behan
was working as a free-lance journalist, "to get enough money to
finish my novel in peace", anticipating a final draft by Christmas
(1952).[37] He wrote Vail in October that he had 50,000 words on
paper.[38] (50,000 words, very roughly, is half the size of the final
version; yet Behan showed Hamilton only thirty pages in Dublin.
Possibly it was an expression of Behan's confidence in the quality
of that "bit that I am not ashamed of", "Bridewell Revisited".)
Almost exactly six years after his letter to Vail, *Borstal Boy* was
published in Britain. The reviews, for the most part, were highly
favourable, and the first printing of 15,000 copies was quickly
sold out.[39] The book was banned in the Republic of Ireland (a copy
was sent to the Censorship Board by a fellow Dublin author),[40] and
in New Zealand and Australia.

It was a time of production, celebrity, achievement, Behan's
autumn 1958. *The Hostage*, most popular of his plays, premiered
on 14 October; *Borstal Boy* was published a week later, and rehearsals were commencing in New York for *The Quare Fellow*
(where it would win an "Obie" award). And now, just when his
career blossomed and there was wide spread appreciation of his
talent, it all started to spiral downward. But that's another story.

The Irish ban on *Borstal Boy* was eventually lifted, six years after
Behan's death; but it was a censored version (omitting the rude
lyrics, pages 335–38, and 351) that was allowed into the country.[41]
In 1967 the state subsidised Abbey Theatre presented a dramatised
version of the book—at the time, the book itself was still banned
in Ireland—and it proved one of their most popular successes.

Behan manuscripts are hard to come by. Many that were not destroyed have subsequently been lost. Those in Morris Library form an exceptional resource on the evolution of *Borstal Boy*, and of its author—the sixteen-odd years between "The Courteous Borstal" and *Borstal Boy* being, in essence, the extent of Brendan Behan's creative life.

* * *

viii. Borstal Boy: A Portrait of the Artist as a Young Prisoner by *Colbert Kearney**

At first sight, Brendan Behan's *Borstal Boy* seems to be devoid of any structure other than simple chronology, yet this apparent carelessness is the disarming deception of the storyteller, one of the means by which the narrator makes us believe in the entirely spontaneous truth of his tale. It is quite easy to establish that the work does not contain the whole historical truth, the truth of fact, and, far from being a piece of spontaneous recounting, is the result of many beginnings and revisions. What the novel does contain is the truth of fiction: the penal institutions bear much the same relationship to *Borstal Boy* as the island does to *Robinson Crusoe*. Beneath the illusion of actuality is a structure which expresses the development of a personality. *Borstal Boy* is a work of creative autobiography, that *genre* in which the author scrutinises his formative years in the light of his later vision of himself. True to the style and scope of an oral delivery—which the novel pretends to be—the structure consists of a series of unmaskings: the narrator is perpetually posing and examining the pose. The young lad who is arrested in Liverpool has very definite views of himself and his role; these have undergone many painful changes by the time he returns to Dublin.

Asked to single out the most characteristic note of Irish poetry, Professor Sean Lucy chose what he termed "dramatic self-awareness":

* *Ariel: A Review of International English Literature* (Calgary, Alberta), VII, No. 2 (April 1976), 47–62.

something which for good or ill contains the power and appetite to see ourselves, and those things and people that catch our imagination, in terms of dynamic, imaginatively-compelling role.[42]

This self-awareness is the essential element in Behan's style. It can be shown that the tradition out of which he wrote was the native Irish tradition which, deprived of libraries and printing presses, survived in oral form.[43] Reading *Borstal Boy* is like being in the audience at a live performance. The *seanchai*, the Gaelic story-teller, commands attention not merely by relating but also by re-enacting; he achieves depth not by commentary or analysis but by the dramatic power of his performance. In his presence one is close to the primal roots of drama.

In 1939, aged sixteen, Behan travelled to England to strike a blow for Ireland by disrupting the British war-effort with bombs. His action was not sanctioned by the I.R.A. leadership and was against the advice of family and friends. He was tailed on arrival by the Liverpool police and the novel opens as the detectives enter Behan's digs and catch him about to throw his bomb-making equipment out the window.

The unofficial nature of the invasion is not mentioned in the book where Behan presents himself as the traditional volunteer under arrest, making the customary statement of loyalty to the cause and defiance of the Crown. He is surprised at the lack of reaction from his captors but comforts himself by imagining the re-ception at home:

> The left-wing element in the movement would be delighted, and the others, the craw-thumpers, could not say anything against me, because I was a good Volunteer, captured carrying the struggle to England's doorstep. . . .[44]

He acts out his role as a "felon of our land", a role immortalised in legend and in the prison memoirs of men like John Mitchel and Tom Clarke. He ends his statement with the scaffold-cry of the Manchester Martyrs, "God save Ireland", and the memory of the ballad which commemorates them enables him to look defiance at his captors:

> Girt around by cruel foes
> Still their courage proudly rose
> As they thought of them that loved them far and near,
> Of the millions true and brave

> O'er the stormy ocean's wave,
> And our friends in Holy Ireland, ever dear.

He relishes the mental picture of his friends:

> And all the people at home would say, reading the papers, "Ah, sure, God help poor Brendan, wasn't I only talking to him a week ago?" "By Jasus, he was a great lad all the same, and he only sixteen." (p. 13)

The seriousness of his situation in Lime Street Station is almost lost sight of as his imagination feasts on the traditional rewards of his position.

As long as he can assume this role in full, he is capable of taking whatever abuse is offered him, but when the cell door is closed he finds himself physically cold, uncomfortable, lonely. His role or projected self is under pressure and the adolescent seeks release in masturbation.

> I . . . wondered if anyone else has done it in the same condition. I didn't like to mention them by name, even in my mind. Some of them had left the cell for the rope or the firing squad. (p. 16)

During the first few hours of his glorious martyrdom he is haunted by the very shades who had supported him during the initial interrogation: they remind him that the traditional Volunteer should be able to resist the temptations of the flesh.

While growing up, Behan had assumed that since the I.R.A. Volunteer was fighting for Ireland against England he could count on the support of all Irishmen and the opposition of all Englishmen. His political education and his reading of Republican prisoners' memoirs would have instilled into him an insistence on his status as a political rather than a common prisoner: traditionally the Volunteer listed among the hardships of prison life the contact with criminals, the scum of England's gutter. Behan soon discovers that such assumptions are hard to retain. One of his captors is from Munster with obvious Irish accent and name, Larry Houlihan, but despite his origins (or, perhaps, because of them) Houlihan goes out of his way to treat the Irish prisoner with special harshness. On the other hand there was Charlie, one of the common criminals, a sailor who was later to be killed in a convoy. Charlie came from a London suburb but showed more fellow-feeling with Behan than did the Irish constable. Behan and Charlie become "chinas" (mates), despite the fact that as I.R.A. Volunteer and Royal Navy seaman they are technically at war with each other.

The young prisoner's confusion is not limited to questions of nationality unless, in the Irish context, religion be considered an aspect of nationality. Despite numerous confrontations and ex-communications, the average Volunteer was a staunch Catholic and Behan, though not ostentatious in his religious observances, was essentially a devout Catholic. In the gloom and isolation of his cell, he wonders if he will be able to attend mass. (He assumes that the priest will be Irish.) His spirits rise as he follows the mass —without a book, he adds proudly—and he loses his loneliness in communion with the universal church. It was "like being let to the warmth of a big turf fire this cold Sunday morning" (p. 63). Benediction affords him an opportunity to raise his fine singing voice in clouds of incense and nostalgia and he returns to his cell a much happier boy.

> There was a black dark frost outside, and the cocoa was smashing and warm. It was now four o'clock and the biggest part of the week-end punched in, thanks be to God. (p. 67)

Nor is the sense of communion confined to the chapel: Charlie has solemnly declared that, despite the fact that some of the warders and prisoners have it in for Behan because of his membership of the I.R.A., he remains Behan's china. However, this new sense of buoyancy is not to last.

Behan is pleased when ordered to see the Catholic chaplain but is shocked to be greeted with a list of charges against the I.R.A. and an ultimatum to choose between it and the Catholic church. Behan loses his temper and replies with a catalogue of the despotic tendencies of the hierarchy. For insulting a Catholic priest he is beaten up by Protestant warders and he realises that he is being punished by one element of the prison establishment for insubordination to another. Prison regulations required that all prisoners attend the services of the religion listed on their papers and thus the priest is powerless to excommunicate Behan effectively. Religious services were popular among prisoners as a means of breaking the monotony of their lives and the most popular of all was the Friday night religious instruction for R.C.'s which was conducted around the basis of many prisoners' dreams, an open fire. Behan brought his chair as closely as he could to the fire and other prisoners very kindly make room for him. Ensconced in such luxury, he is incapable of bearing malice and he tells himself that perhaps the priest was not altogether bad but merely doing his duty as he thought best. Then a warder taps him on the shoulder and he is told that, on the priest's instructions, he is to be returned to his cell. The effect is traumatic. He could survive beatings, abuse, solitary confinement but this rejection is different and he is close to tears for the first time in years. He recalls the kindness he had received as a child from Sister Monica and Father Campbell and bitterly reminds himself that he must forget it and all that it meant for him.

> Wasn't I the soft eedgit all the same, to expect anything more off that fat bastard of a drurid? Weren't the priests famous for backing up the warders even the time of the Fenians? When Dr. Gallagher was driven mad in Chatham Prison.

> But I wouldn't always be inside, and if I could do the like of Father Lane an ill turn in my turn, by Jesus and I'd be the boy to do it.

> Let them come to me some time at home with their creeping Jesus old gab, I'd say to them: what about this night in Walton Jail, you bastards? (p. 104)

(This is perhaps the only instance in the entire book of unadulterated bitterness.) In the allusion to Tom Clarke's account of the fate of Dr. Gallagher we notice Behan retreating for protection into the role of "felon of our land", a role which we have already seen to be under considerable strain.

His altercation with the priest brings him a beating followed by solitary confinement on bread and water. Unwilling to earn another beating for defiance, he paces his cell singing to himself.

> Some in the convict's dreary cell
> Have found a living tomb,
> And some unseen untended fell
> Within the dungeon's gloom,
> But what care we, although it be
> Trod by a ruffian band,
> God bless the clay where rest today
> The Felons of our Land.

Then the martyr's nose detects the food of which he is deprived and once again the spirit grapples with the flesh. He catches the

112

mental torture, as he often does, by following the soul-stirring purity of the ballad with a more worldly rhapsody:

Wasn't it the great pity that the fellow that was doing the suffering couldn't be where the singing was to get the benefit of it. Mother of Christ, wasn't there a thousand places between Belfast and Bantry Bay where a fellow would be stuffed with grub, not to mind dowsed in porter, if he could only be there and here at the same time? But I supposed that would be like trying to get a drink at your own funeral. Make way there, you with the face, and let in the man that's doing jail for Ireland, and suffering hunger and abuse, let him up to the bar there. Oh, come up at once, the publican would say, what kind of men are you at all? Have you no decency of spirit about you, that wouldn't make way for one of the Felons of our Land? Come on, son, till herself gives you this plate of bacon and cabbage, and blessings of Jesus on you, and on everyone like you. It's my own dinner I'm giving you, for you were not expected and you among that parcel of white-livered, thin-lipped, paper-waving, key-rattling hangmen. And, come on; after your dinner there's a pint to wash it down, aye, and a glass of malt if you fancy it. Give us up a song there. Yous have enough of songs out of yous about the boys that faced the Saxon foe, but, bejasus, when there's one of them here among you, the real Ally Daly, the real goat's genollickers, yous are as silent as the tomb. Sing up, yous whores gets. (p. 93)

And so, drunk and happy on this massacre of matter by mind, the prisoner's imagination rises and swells to the tune of "Out and Make Way for the Bold Fenian Men". Yet, as the prisoner is only too painfully aware, spiritual victories seldom last very long, despite the presence of the ghost of Terence MacSweeney, who starved for seventy-eight days, looking down on his petty privations. Volunteer Behan knows what is expected of him; he also knows what he would do if a warder were to tempt him to sing "God Save the King" by offering him a round steak:

Jesus, Mary, and Joseph, he'd be a lucky man that I didn't take the hand and all off him. And sing a High Mass, never mind a couple of lines of "God Save the King", for it, aye or for the half of it. (p. 96)

Two months in Walton Gaol had led him to question some of the extreme aspects of his career as a Republican felon. He had not changed his opinion on British imperialism but was willing to settle for a tactical retreat from an exposed position. He would have his revenge outside; till then he did not wish to draw unnecessary attention to himself. This is presented with hilarious clarity in his encounter with Callan, a Republican from Monaghan.

Despite the fact that he was imprisoned for the theft of an overcoat, Callan was a Volunteer of extreme rigidity. No longer a believer in the brotherhood of all Irishmen, Behan finds Callan a fanatical and humourless fool who stupidly invites the warders' wrath. Nevertheless, Callan is a genuine member of the I.R.A. and this cannot be ignored. The encounter with Callan coincides with a period of great danger for Behan. In Coventry, two I.R.A. Volunteers were under sentence of death for bombing offences; anti-Irish feeling is so high that Behan's chinas, Charlie and Ginger, stick close to him to prevent a sudden attack. Callan proposes a demonstration of solidarity with the condemned Volunteers; Behan considers this futile, leading to nothing more than an increase in hostility and a beating from the warders. Behan is ashamed of his own fears but the desire for self-preservation is uppermost in his mind. He tries to lose himself in the comfortable triviality of Mrs. Gaskell's *Cranford* but his escape is shattered by Callan's voice tearing through the prison. He calls on Behan to demonstrate his faith in the Republic. Behan, frightened out of his wits, curses Callan and the Republic and the overcoat which brought himself and Callan together. He will grant Callan's courage but wishes to be excused from any heroics himself. To Callan's repeated cries, Behan replies with a "discreet shout" and jumps back into bed. Questioned by the warders, he replies meekly that he is reading; then he listens to the groans of suffering as Callan is beaten up by the warders.

The executions are due to take place the following morning. As usual in Behan's writings, sparse prose is a sign of deep emotion.

> A church bell rang out a little later. They are beginning to die now, said I to myself. As it chimed the hour, I bent my forehead to my handcuffed right hand and made the Sign of the Cross by moving my head and chest along my outstretched fingers. It was the best that I could do. (p. 143)

Lurking in the last sentence is the uncomfortable knowledge that his behaviour, no matter how defensible, had fallen short of that prescribed for a "felon of our land".

Walton Gaol proved a hard school; Behan was perhaps lucky to escape with his life. His view of himself in terms of national and religious ideals has had to concede a great deal. Yet he realises that no matter how much he may be forced to give in this respect, it would be disastrous to give anything in the purely physical arena. When victimised by another prisoner he knows that he must either assert himself or go under. But what self? As his masks have been shattered one by one, he falls back on his ultimate identity.

> I was no country Paddy from the middle of the Bog of Allen to be frightened to death by a lot of Liverpool seldom-fed bastards, nor was I one of your wrap-the-green-flag-round-me junior Civil Servants that came into the I.R.A. from the Gaelic League, and well ready to die for their country any day of the week, purity in their hearts, truth on their lips, for the glory of God and the honour of Ireland. No, be Jesus, I was from Russell Street, North Circular Road, Dublin, from the Northside, where, be Jesus, the likes of Dale wouldn't make a dinner for them, where the whole of this pack of Limeys would be scruff-hounds, would be et, bet, and threw up again—et without salt. I'll James you, you bastard. (p. 86)

Thus roused, he attacks his taunter with a sewing-needle and, luckily for himself, he does his damage and is arrested by warders before the victim's gang can avenge the assault. He accepts his punishment with ease, knowing that his newly acquired reputation as a tough guy is an insurance policy against utter loss of face and identity. It is a savage method but one dictated by an environment in which the brutality of warders is taken for granted and in which a prisoner is cruelly slashed with a razor on suspicion of stealing cigarette-butts. Seeing the slashed prisoner, Behan ponders his own shortcomings as "a fearless rebel" (p. 109).

There is a positive side to his development which now begins to emerge. He has a Crusoe-like capacity for enjoyment: prison food is often described with a relish normally reserved for more imaginative cuisine, reading a book is made to seem a feast, a mishap to a member of the staff provokes an orgy of pleasure. Yet his greatest gift is his humour and his greatest delight is in friendship. Having broken through the clouds of nationalism, he senses the strong fellow-feeling between himself and the English boys, especially those from urban backgrounds. This is underlined at the end of the first section when we meet a sad character named Hartigan,

115

Liverpool-Irish, son of a Catholic from the west of Ireland. Hartigan assumes that he and Behan will be chinas, but Behan has rejected such assumptions and remains with the more congenial Charlie and Ginger. He himself had entered Walton Gaol like Hartigan, lonely and seeking solace in his Irishness, but two months had taught him a lot.

The most striking element in the second section of the novel is the undisguised boyish joy with which Behan and his friends greet the change from the violence of Walton to the more liberal regime at Feltham Boys' Prison. The journey is described in language which reminds one of boarding-school vacations; there is plenty of food at Feltham and, luxury of extravagant luxuries, Behan is given his first pair of pyjamas. He finds little difficulty in joining with the other boys who were, despite superficial differences, essentially of the same background as himself. He warms to the wit of the Londoner's rhyming slang; they enjoy his colourful *dublinese*. Linguistic dexterity and musical ability stand him in good stead and he is happy that most of his fellow-young-prisoners are not particularly interested in the nature of his offence—some of them cannot get the initials I.R.A. in the correct order.

A certain amount of conflict remains. Another I.R.A. prisoner urges Behan to adopt a superior attitude to the common criminals. This prisoner is generous with gifts and advice: Behan accepts the gifts and rejects the advice for he finds the person unattractive, sound as a Volunteer but deficient in the spirit and sense of humour which enables people to live with each other. Although there is no explicit comment, Behan is puzzled to discover he has more in common with a Cockney thief than with this Volunteer. He refused to join in Callan's demonstration on the grounds that he was afraid of being beaten up; yet he is willing to risk being beaten to support his china, Charlie. With the Londoners he can swap childhood memories of hawking-cries, football matches, horse-racing lore; with them he shares a grudge against the ruling classes. (Some prisoners suggest that Behan might make better use of his knowledge of explosives in the houses of the aristocracy.) He has found his place among his fellows and when one tries to stir up feeling against him because of his membership of the I.R.A., Behan easily dismisses him by calling him an informer, the lowest form of prison life.

This new sense of integration flowers into one of the great set-pieces of comic literature, Holy Week at Feltham. The narrator would have us believe that being excommunicated enabled him to relish the incidents with atheistic objectivity, but this does not convince us. He is still sufficiently religious to have qualms about loose behaviour in church and, when he finds himself lapsing into the liturgy, he must remind himself to be disrespectful. In fact, what raises this episode above farce and into the realm of high comedy is the strong undercurrent of genuine religious feeling which informs it.

As we have seen, prisoners looked forward to religious services as a break and it is not surprising that non-Catholics envied the Catholics their long Easter Week ceremonies. Behan, a catholic Catholic, sees no just reason why his unfortunate heretical friends should be deprived on a technicality, of the opportunity for spiritual exercise and so he becomes a missionary, guiding a mixed bunch of pagans, protestants, atheists and agnostics into the Church on a week's free trial with no obligation to join. They are received as prison regulations demand, that is, strictly regulated according to the amount of tobacco each was allowed: remand prisoners (own clothes, twenty a day, unlimited parcels) sat in front, those in solitary confinement (nothing) sat at the back, the others ranged in between. The neo-Catholics show an immediate and expert understanding of Jesus' suffering; after all, he was, like themselves, a criminal arrested on information received, charged and convicted in very unfair circumstances. With utter conviction they abuse the informer, Judas, and warmly approve of Peter's desire to inflict grievous bodily harm on him. "Carve the bastard up." The essence of the comedy is not any disrespectful rowdyism but the lively religious link between Jesus aud the prisoners: they show an awareness of the story more informed, intense and imaginative than that normally found in "outside" churches. They are the lost ones for whom Jesus expressed special concern.

On Good Friday, the Italian priest, equally carried away by the Passion, asks the prisoners to accompany him round the Stations of the Cross. The warders were dumbfounded at the breach of the regulations but helpless against the command of the priest. As the prisoners mingle in a new communal ecstasy, those that have minister unto those that have not. The pastoral reputation of the Catholic Church was never so high and the amazing priest who is partly responsible for this glimpse of paradise is very properly rewarded in the little final paragraph which encapsulates the uplift of heart which our hero has enjoyed at Feltham:

> On Easter Sunday the little priest skipped around the altar like a spring lamb and gave a triumphant sermon in gleaming white and gold vestments and the sun shining through the window on him. (p. 201)

The novel takes its title from the third and final section which deals with the time spent in Hollesley Bay Borstal Institution. On the way there the boys smoke and sing and fly streamers. Behan sings both popular and patriotic songs to the appreciation of his fellow-prisoners. He feels no need to conceal his membership of the I.R.A. and when he gives a fervently obscene account of the damage inflicted by the I.R.A. on a Black and Tan column outside the town of Macroom his English pals admire the wit and applaud the insubordination.

Inevitably almost, one reminds oneself that these boys have been declared unfit for human society. Behan does not consider himself a criminal and his friends are singularly free from the remorse of conscience which their confinement is intended to excite. Behan remarks that a prisoner's crime was only alluded to, like the colour of his hair or his place of origin, as a means of description. A more amusing expression of this most Christian charity emerges in the tale of the boy, imprisoned for forgery, who won the cross-country race in an unusual manner:

> . . . the long forger's legs of him and his beaky counterfeit nose brought him in before anyone else, also due to the conservation of his energies behind the incinerators, where he slyly hid and rested himself while the other honest poor bastards—well, by comparison, poor simple robbers and rapers and murderers—went round the second time. (p. 279)

All objection is overruled because the majority feeling is that he has deserved his fifty cigarettes prize for his cunning if not for his athletical prowess. Without condoning murder, rape or forgery, one cannot but feel for these boys. They react to their environment. In Walton Gaol one had to be vicious to survive; in the more enlightened atmosphere of Borstal the behaviour is proportionately more civilised. For most of these boys, the governor of Borstal was their first contact with an authority they could respect. Hollesley Bay was something of a boarding-school: there are abuses and punishments but, despite the fact that it is an open Borstal, only one boy tries to escape.

The escaper functions in the novel in a manner similar to Hartigan in the opening section: in analysing him and his condition, Behan tells us a good deal about himself. The escaper is an upper-class "toff" who suffers more than most because he is isolated in a mainly working-class milieu.

> He was dead lonely; more lonely than I and with more reason. The other fellows might give me a rub about Ireland or about the bombing campaign, and that was seldom enough, and I was never short of an answer, historically informed and obscene, for them. But I was nearer to them than they would ever let Ken be. I had the same rearing as most of them, Dublin, Liverpool, Manchester, Glasgow, London. All our mothers had all done the pawn—pledging on Monday, releasing on Saturday. We all knew the chip shop and the picture house, and the fourpenny rush of a Saturday afternoon, and the summer swimming in the canal and being chased along the railway by the cops. (p. 241)

Remembering his own isolation, Behan sympathises with the lonely aristocrat, even when it displeases his own chinas.

The question of class becomes prominent in this section. (On his arrest in Liverpool, Behan had made left-wing noises but in retrospect we see that they were part of his original pose; they were not the result of intellectual analysis, which is understandable when one remembers that he was only sixteen.) In Borstal he has a series of political discussions with a socialist from Blackpool who is imprisoned because he strangled his girl-friend, an action which is criticised by the normally uncritical prisoners and which Behan is forced to admit was "a bit stern all right" (p. 306). This socialist engages Behan in some of the very rare intellectual argument of the book. He sympathises with the people of Ireland but condemns the I.R.A. for failing to see that their fight was not with England but with the class-structure. He urges Behan, a member of the working class, to consider himself above the other prisoners who would steal rather than work and who are, eventually, "a dirty degenerate lot of scum" (p. 303).

Behan seems unable to counter these arguments in intellectual terms—which is surprising when one considers his consistent pride in his intelligence and loquacity—but his emotions refuse to allow him to reject his chinas. In his heart he knows that there might be deficiencies in the social theory of a person who strangled his own girl-friend and, as usual, the eventual condemnation is based on the socialist's lack of humour, implying as it does the lack of understanding and charity. Despite his belief in the brotherhood of workers, he is a loner; Behan is not his china.

> Nor is anyone else your china, said I, in my own mind. And small blame to them, with your scrawny face and your red Anti-Christ's stubble on it, and the miserable undertaker's labourer's chat out of you . . . I had no mother to break her heart, and I had no china to take my part, but I had one friend and a girl was she, that I croaked with her own silk stocking. (p. 355)

Nevertheless, the socialist has helped Behan clarify his opinions: when accused by a Scot of liking the English despite their behaviour in Ireland, he replies that it is the imperialist system which is offensive in Ireland and that some of its most obnoxious lackeys are Irish and Scots.

The news of his release comes as a surprise both to Behan and to the reader. The boy at boarding-school will count the last few weeks, days, hours and minutes, but Behan does not. Also, the first duty of a prisoner of war is to escape; Behan claims that the odds against success were enormous but one feels that this is not the whole truth. Gradually one comes to the strange conclusion that the prisoner has enjoyed his prison. The governor claims that Borstal has made a man of Behan, a claim that is not disputed. It has certainly taught him a great deal about himself and about life in general: it has sharpened his perception, taught him to use his comic gifts as a means of survival, granted him leisure to read widely and given him his first literary award. Some years later he wrote of a book:

> I read this book a lot of years before it was in Penguins, at a time when I was leading a more contemplative life and had plenty of time to think about what I read.[45]

The irony does not conceal the truth and one notices the pride in an *alma mater* which provided such education even in pre-Penguin days.

Behan's farewells are quick, the sparse prose being the sign of deep and tender emotion. It is more like a prize-pupil leaving school than a prisoner being deported. In Dublin Bay he counts the hills and the spires of the city, remarking that they were as if he never left them. This is a complex observation, part of the complexity being the surprise that such things could have stayed the same when he had changed so much. He is uncertain what other changes await him: the immigration official welcomes him quietly in Irish, the detective on the gangway says nothing.

NOTES

1 The others were edited by either his publishers or, in the case of his major plays, the theatrical managements or their associates. With some of the books this involved no more than correcting spelling and typing errors, adding translations for the odd phrases in Irish—making minor clarifications. The work required for the tape-recorded books, however, and for the final version of *The Hostage* was considerable.

2 Conversations with Beatrice Behan and others. Dublin, April 1974.

3 I am indebted for many of the biographical details to: Seamus de Burca, *Brendan Behan: A Memoir* (Newark, Delaware: Proscenium Press, 1971); Ted E. Boyle, *Brendan Behan* (New York: Twayne, 1969).

4 Sean Kavanagh, "In Prison", in *The World of Brendan Behan*, ed. Sean McCann (New York: Twayne, 1966), pp. 67–69.

5 Letter from Brendan Behan to Bob Bradshaw, 4 December 1943; located in Fales Library, New York University.

6 De Burca, p. 16.

7 All page numbers for *Borstal Boy* refer to the edition published by Alfred A. Knopf, New York, 1959.

8 Arthur Gelb, "Brendan Behan's Sober Side", *New York Times*, 18 September 1960, p. 3x.

9 Letter from Behan to Bradshaw.

10 Ibid.

11 See Catherine Rynne, "The Behan We Knew", *The World of Brendan Behan*, pp. 180–81 and 186.

12 Ulick O'Connor, *Brendan Behan* (Englewood Cliffs: Prentice Hall, 1971), p. 55.

13 The character's name, in the book, is Ken Jones (see especially page 234). In an extract published earlier, in *New Statesman* (see below), he was called Kenneth Large, and was "in" for "driving a motor car into his father".

14 Dominic Behan, *My Brother Brendan* (New York: Simon and Schuster, 1965), p. 117.

15 Rynne, pp. 180–81.

16 Beatrice Behan, *My Life With Brendan* (London: Leslie Frewin, 1973), p. 67.

17 Rae Jeffs, *Brendan Behan: Man and Showman* (Cleveland: World, 1968), pp. 21, 33, and 39.

18 Ibid., p. 41.

19 See Beatrice Behan, pp. 133–34.

20 Ibid., p. 99.

21 Jeffs, p. 22.

22 Ibid.

23 52 (8 December, 1956), 740.

24 Brendan Behan, "Letters from Ireland", *Points*, no. 15 (Autumn 1952), 71.

25 Ibid.

26 Boyle, p. 103 and p. 105.

27 Reference to Toller's *The Book of Swallows*, poems he wrote while in jail.

28 Jeffs, p. 38.

29 Gerard Fay, "Mr. Behan's Public School" [review of *Borstal Boy*], *Manchester Guardian*, 21 October 1958, p. 4.

30 "Letters from Ireland", p. 71.

31 "Pharos", "A Spectators' Notebook", 14 November 1958, p. 635.

32 "Borstal Boy" [letter to the editor], *Spectator*, 21 November 1958, p. 703. Lusty wrote that he was now convinced the alteration, "on a very few difficult occasions", had been a mistake and that a subsequent edition would rectify this. But this would have little effect over all.

33 Beatrice Behan, p. 99.

34 Jeffs, pp. 23–31 and 33–34.

35 Ibid., p. 31.

36 Walter Hackett, "The Behan" [obituary], *Washington Post*, 22 March 1964, *Show* supplement, p. G–1.

37 "Letters from Ireland", pp. 71–72.

38 Ibid., p. 74.

39 Jeffs, pp. 72–73.

40 Timothy Patrick Coogan, *Ireland Since the Rising* (New York: Praeger, 1966), p. 171.

41 Corgi Books [paperback] (London, 1961). I am not clear if the 1961 printing was censored or not, but the edition on sale in Dublin in the spring of 1974—the second Corgi reprinting of 1970—certainly was.

42 *Irish Poets in English* (The Thomas Davis Lectures on Anglo-Irish Poetry), edited by Sean Lucy (Cork and Dublin: Mercier Press, 1973), p. 27.

43 I hope to show this in a later essay.

44 *Borstal Boy* (London: Corgi, 1961), p. 13. Subsequent page references are to this edition.

45 *Hold Your Hour and Have Another* (London: Hutchinson, 1963), p. 189.

7

The Hostage

i. New Amalgam by *Kenneth Tynan**

At the end of N. F. Simpson's *A Resounding Tinkle* there is a section, aberrantly omitted from the Royal Court production, in which four B.B.C. critics discuss the play. It reads, in part:

> *Chairman:* Denzil Pepper—what do you make of this?
> *Pepper:* This is a hotchpotch. I think that emerges quite clearly. The thing has been thrown together—a veritable rag-bag of last year's damp fireworks, if a mixed metaphor is in order.
> *Miss Salt:* Yes, I suppose it *is* what we must call a hotchpotch. I do think, though—accepting Denzil Pepper's definition—I do think, and this is the point I feel we ought to make, it is, surely, isn't it, an *inspired* hotchpotch.
> *Pepper:* A hotchpotch de luxe. . . . A theatrical haggis.
> *Chairman:* Isn't this what our ancestors would have delighted in calling a gallimaufry?
> *(Pause.)*
> *Mustard:* Yes. I'm not sure that I don't prefer the word gallimaufry to Denzil Pepper's hodge-podge.
> *Pepper:* Hotchpotch. No, I stick, quite unrepentantly, to my own word. . . .

The satanic accuracy of all this is enough to make any critic's elbow fly defensively up. I quote it because it has a chilling relevance to Brendan Behan's *The Hostage* (Theatre Royal, Stratford E.). He would, I fancy, be a pretty perjured critic who could swear that no such thoughts infested his mind while watching Mr. Behan's new (careful now)—Mr. Behan's new *play*. I use the word advisedly, and have since sacked my advisers: for conventional terminology is totally inept to describe the uses to which Mr. Behan and his director, Joan Littlewood, are trying to put the theatre. The old pigeonholes will no longer serve.

* The *Observer* (London), (19 October 1958), p. 19.

From a critic's point of view, the history of twentieth-century drama is the history of a collapsing vocabulary. Categories that were formerly thought sacred and separate began to melt and flow together, like images in a dream. Reaching, to steady himself, for words and concepts that had withstood the erosion of centuries, the critic found himself, more often than not, clutching a handful of dust.

Already, long before 1900, tragedy and comedy had abandoned the pretence of competition and become a double act, exchanging their masks so rapidly that the effort of distinguishing one from the other was at best a pedantic exercise. Farce and satire, meanwhile, were miscegenating as busily as ever, and both were conducting affairs on the side with revue and musical comedy. Opera, with Brecht and Weill, got in on everybody's act; and vaudeville, to cap everything, started to flirt with tragi-comedy in *Waiting for Godot* and *The Entertainer*.

The critic, to whom the correct assignment of compartments is as vital as it is to the employees of Wagons-Lits, reeled in poleaxed confusion. What had happened was that multi-party drama was moving towards coalition government. Polonius did not know the half of it: a modern play can, if it wishes, be tragical-comical-historical-pastoral-farcical-satirical-operatical-musical-music - hall, in any combination or all at the same time. And it is only because we have short memories that we forget that a phrase already exists to cover all these seemingly disparate breeds. It is Commedia dell' Arte. *The Hostage* is a Commedia dell' Arte production.

Its theme is Ireland, seen through the bloodshot prism of Mr. Behan's talent. The action, which is noisy and incessant, takes place in a Dublin lodging-house owned by a Blimpish veteran of the Troubles whose Anglophobia is so devout that he calls himself Monsieur instead of Mr. His caretaker is Pat (Howard Goorney), a morose braggart who feels that all the gaiety departed from the cause of Irish liberty when the I.R.A. became temperate, dedicated and holy.

Already, perhaps, this sounds like a normal play; and it may well sound like a tragedy when I add that the plot concerns a kidnapped Cockney soldier who is threatened with death unless his opposite number, an I.R.A. prisoner sentenced to be hanged, is reprieved. Yet there are, in this production, more than twenty songs, many of them blasphemously or lecherously gay, and some of them sung by the hostage himself. Authorship is shared by Mr. Behan, his uncle, and "Trad". Nor can one be sure how much of the dialogue is pure Behan and how much is gifted embroidery; for the whole production sounds spontaneous, a communal achievement based on Miss Littlewood's idea of theatre as a place where people talk to people, not actors to audiences. As with Brecht, actors step in and out of character so readily that phrases like "dramatic unity" are ruled out of court: we are simply watching a group of human beings who have come together to tell a lively story in speech and song.

Some of the speech is brilliant mock-heroic; some of it is merely crude. Some of the songs are warmly ironic (e.g., "There's no place on earth like the world"); others are more savagely funny. Some of the acting (Avis Bunnage, Clive Barker) is sheer vaudeville; some of it (Murray Melvin as the captive and Celia Salkeld as the country girl whom, briefly and abruptly, he loves) is tenderly realistic. The work ends in a mixed, happy jabber of styles, with a piano playing silent-screen music while the Cockney is rescued and accidentally shot by one of the lodgers, who defiantly cries, in the last line to be audibly uttered: "I'm a secret policeman, and I don't care who knows it!"

Inchoate and naïve as it often is, this is a prophetic and joyously exciting evening. It seems to be Ireland's function, every twenty years or so, to provide a playwright who will kick English drama from the past into the present. Mr. Behan may well fill the place vacated by Sean O'Casey.

Perhaps more important, Miss Littlewood's production is a boisterous premonition of something we all want—a biting popular drama that does not depend on hit songs, star names, spa sophistication or the more melodramatic aspects of homosexuality. Sean Kenny's setting, a skeleton stockade of a bedroom surrounded by a towering blind alley of slum windows, is, as often at this theatre, by far the best in London.

*   *   *

ii. Go-As-You-Please by *J. C. Trewin**

If *Uncle Dundo* is go-as-you-please comedy within a familiar frame, Brendan Behan's *The Hostage* (Theatre Royal, Stratford, E.) is a go-as-you-please invention without any special boundary. We know from *The Quare Fellow* that Behan has an Irish foam of phrase. In this new piece it froths unchecked across and around the dubious Dublin lodging-house in which a young British soldier is being held hostage. If a member of the I.R.A. is executed in Belfast, there must be a reprisal, and here is the victim.

That sounds like a terrifying subject, and we know how Joseph O'Connor dealt with a similar situation in "The Iron Harp". But Behan uses it to laugh at I.R.A. discipline, social work, anything he feels like discussing at the drop of a hat. The piece seems indeed to be extemporised as the actors speak. There is a good deal of swift Irish talk, some of it better than the rest, and when he feels that there is need for a change Behan will let the actors carry on with a ballad or so ("Most of the songs were written by the author, some of the others were written by his uncle. The rest are traditional Irish, or are borrowed from the repertoire of the music-hall.") Now and again seriousness breaks in; but my general impression of *The Hostage* is that Behan much prefers laughter, and that the semi-tragic ending is something tacked on almost as an afterthought. I say "semi-tragic" because the corpse (the Cockney boy has been shot accidentally) rises in a green light to join with the rest of the cast in singing "The bells of Hell go ting-a-ling-a-ling."

It is nowhere near the O'Casey theatre; still, as a capricious exercise in folk-drama (with Brechtian influences) it has its amusing side, and Joan Littlewood makes one of her most successful and relishing productions. She has players (Howard Goorney and Murray Melvin, for example) who are excellently relaxed and true; and my principal regret is that there is so little of the Irish spirit in a company that does not seem to have been very close to Dublin.

* The *Illustrated London News*, CCXXXIII (1 November 1958), 764.

*   *   *

iii. *The Hostage* by *Thomas Kilroy**

The same central tragic theme is in no better focus in Mr. Behan's by now, very well-known play *The Hostage*. In spite of its Gaelic original, *The Hostage* is quite obviously a product of London's Theatre Workshop and, more particularly of Joan Littlewood whose dynamic direction alone could carry a play like this. Under the encouragement of this experimental theatre Mr. Behan has written a form of intimate, conversational drama where the central theme is lost, apparently without very many regrets, under profuse public-house jokery. On the printed page without the animation of the players Mr. Behan's jokes begin to pall after the first few pages. His scene is set in a Dublin brothel, where prostitutes, homosexuals, pimps, religious maniacs and members of the Irish Republican Army cavort in Mr. Behan's confusion of balladry and bawdiness.

It might all be very exciting for the jaded spirits that seem to fill most of the London theatres to-day, but it is very difficult to see what relation it all bears to Ireland, drama or even Life. In order to stimulate his audience still further Mr. Behan decorates his circus with a liberal amount of topical quips on the Royal Family and material from the Wolfenden Report. Mr. Harold Hobson, the distinguished English critic, speaks of *The Hostage* as giving "the impression of a masterpiece", which is very high praise indeed. Perhaps now, remote from the heated performance given to this play on the London stage, threadbare patches, crude assembly work and unworthy "gimmicks" are more apparent. This in turn raises another point, too involved to handle in a review; just how much can an impressive director cover up by bewitching the audience?

As a post-script: it should not be necessary to add that neither of these two[1] plays has any particular significance for or relevance to, modern Ireland and its problems.

* *Studies; An Irish Quarterly Review* (Dublin), XLVIII (Spring 1959), 111–12. This is a review of the published version of the play.

* * *

iv. Libido at Large by *Robert Brustein**

It has been suggested that in *The Hostage* Brendan Behan is trying to "open up the stage", but this is an understatement. He
would like to hack the stage to bits, crunch the proscenium across
his knees, trample the scenery underfoot, and throw debris wildly
in all directions. Like his various prototypes—Jack Falstaff, Harpo
Marx, W. C. Fields, and Dylan Thomas—Behan is pure Libido on a
rampage, mostly in its destructive phase; and if he has not achieved
the Dionysian purity of those eminent anarchists, he is still a welcome presence in our sanctimonious times. In America, comedy
went underground (*i.e.* turned "sick") when the various humane
societies built a protective wall around mankind, for an art form
based on uninhibited abandon and open aggression cannot long
survive the Anti-Defamation League, the N.A.A.C.P., the Legion
of Decency, and McCall's Togetherness, not to mention those
guardians of cultural virtues who now review theatre, movies, and
T.V. for the newspapers. But Behan seems to have crossed the
Atlantic without any significant accommodation to American tastes,
outside of an abrupt conversion from whiskey to homogenised
milk.

For the dramatic bludgeon he has installed at the Cort is now
flailing indiscriminately at everything in sight, including the British
Empire, the I.R.A., the Catholic Church, the Protestant clergy,
the army, the police, the F.B.I., and the D.A.R. What these disparate organisations have in common is their orthodoxy: Behan
is waging total war on all social institutions excepting brothels and
distilleries. But though destructive Libido can be the source of a
lot of fun, it is hardly an organising principle, so the author's
assault on order leaves this play almost totally lacking in dramatic
logic. Its substance is taped together with burlesque routines, Irish
reels, bar-room ballads, and outrageous gags (some old, some new,
some borrowed, but all "blue"), while its scarecrow plot is just a
convenient appendage on which to hang a string of blasphemous
howlers. "This is a serious play!" screams a dour, baleful, humourless I.R.A. officer after a typical irreverency. But he convinces nobody. *The Hostage* is neither serious nor even a play. It is a roaring

* The *New Republic*, CXLIII (3 October 1960), 20–21.

128

vaudeville turn, too disordered to support any more than a wink of solemnity.

Nevertheless, the plot—which is exhausted the moment you sum it up—does seem serious in its basic outline. Set in a Dublin brothel in modern times, the action revolves around the kidnapping, and ultimate death, of a young English soldier, taken by the I.R.A. because the British are going to execute a Belfast revolutionary. This promises an Irish political drama, and one can easily imagine how O'Casey might have interpreted the same situation. The brothel would become a symbolic Temple of Love, Life, and the Dance; the prostitutes would be "pagan girls" with ample bosoms and free, sensual natures; the comic characters would emerge as personifications of bigotry, indifference, and selfishness; the death of the boy would be an occasion for commentary on the victimisation of the innocent by war; and the play would probably conclude with a vision of a better life to come.

But while Behan has turned to O'Casey for his plot outline, he does not share O'Casey's weakness for adolescent sexuality or utopian social communities. In his illogical, irresponsible view of society, in fact, he comes much closer to Ionesco; in his technique and treatment of low life, closer to the early Brecht. His whores are tough, funny, breezy hookers; the brothel is a sleazy dive run exclusively for profit ("Money is the best religion . . . and the best politics"); and the boy's death is followed immediately by his inexplicable resurrection for a final song ("Oh death where is thy sting-a-ling-a-ling"). As for the comics—a grotesque gallery which includes a madam and her "ponce" winging standup jokes at each other in the manner of a minstrel show; a religious eccentric goosed in the middle of her hymn by an ex-Postal clerk with a sanctified air and roaming fingers; and two pansies named Rio Rita and Princess Grace ("That's only my name in religion")—they are on stage primarily for what they can contribute to the general mayhem. For Behan's theme is "Nobody loves you like yourself", and his brothel is simply one of the last refuges of privacy where a man can pursue his pleasures and have his laughs.

On the other hand, the poignancy and desperation of the humour aptly illustrate the growing shakiness of this position as the private world becomes more and more circumscribed. Generously spread throughout the play are topical references which change with the latest newspaper headlines (a Russian sailor off the Baltica is now one of the customers in the house), anxious glances in the direction of the H-bomb ("It's such a big bomb it's after making me scared of little bombs"), and melodious admonitions to Khrushchev, Eisenhower, and Macmillan ("Don't muck about, don't muck about, don't muck about the moon"). The forces gathering outside the brothel have now become so overwhelming that they cannot be ignored; and the violence behind Behan's farcical attitudes reveals his impotent frustration at being involuntarily implicated in the frightening activities of the great powers.

Joan Littlewood's production works hard to preserve all the wilder values of this vaudeville whirligig. The company, which has been mostly imported from her theatre workshop in England, is an excellent one—in the cases of Avis Bunnage, Alfred Lynch, and Patience Collier sometimes even inspired. But while Miss Little-wood has developed the appropriate Epic style, and has scrupu-lously tried to avoid gentility, I still don't think I've really seen the play. Perhaps English actors cannot suppress their instinctive good manners, for while the production rolls along with admirable speed and efficiency, it lacks robustness, coarseness, and true spontaneity. But then only a troupe of burlesque comics endowed with the brutal wit of Simon Dedalus and the shameless vulgarity of Aristophanes could hope to catch the proper tone of this sidewinding improvisa-tion. It is an open question whether *The Hostage* belongs on the legitimate stage at all, but considering that Minsky's is out of business I am very glad to have it there. Its careless laughter is like a sound out of the past, and Behan's paean to unconditioned man is a wholesome antidote to what Orwell called "the smelly little orthodoxies that are now contending for our souls."

*   *   *

v. The Heroic Dimension in Brendan Behan's *The Hostage*
by   *Gordon M. Wickstrom**

Brendan Behan's *The Hostage* is a popular play just now—popu-lar with producing companies and audiences alike. Its mode and

* *Educational Theatre Journal*, XXII (1970), 406–11.

energy are especially appealing to those interested in the new, freer, not-so-literary theatre of the moment. The evolution of the play from the original Gaelic conception, to the English version for Dublin's Abbey, to its fuller development under the direction of Joan Littlewood at her London theatre at Stratford-East is widely known. That the play grew to its present shape out of improvisations by Littlewood's actors, that it still contains open-ended dramatic structures, and has no definitive text demanding respect[2] are features that invite directors to mount original, even eccentric productions for the immediate purposes of particular theatres and audiences. In fact, it is probably impossible to produce *The Hostage* without expanding the scenario to define and clarify certain characters and actions that the text leaves obscure. But this obscurity is only apparent; while Behan leaves the surface data of his dramatic ideas open to invention and improvisation, he is careful enough with his essential drama.

In order to see this drama clearly, we must look past the language, an uncertain element here, and, as though looking through the wrong end of a telescope, watch the action in broadest outline, the diverting detail of its "concatenated events" no longer visible. Paradoxically, the characters, miniaturised by the inverted optics, take on a larger meaning: they now suggest their archetypes and put us on the proper track toward understanding the structure that they represent. *The Hostage* invites us to look for a rhythm and shape built into the spectacle's scenario and residing on the far side of literature where a poetry unique to the theatre lies deeper than the words. This poetry arises from the kind of discoveries that Jerzy Grotowski's actors make as action bombards action, actor confronts character and himself to reveal new elements of myth and emotion in dramatic concert. Ludwik Flaszen writing on Grotowski says, "Theatre starts where the word is not sufficient."[3] Behan's theatre springs from such beginnings, and in *The Hostage* the playwright develops a heroic rhythm not very different from the *tragic rhythm* that Francis Fergusson describes in his *The Idea of a Theater* as the essential of tragic action.

Given these conditions, any production must be controlled by the way in which the director interprets what is the play's most provocative feature: that moment at the end when the hostage, the young British Tommy, Leslie, suddenly comes back to life after he has been accidentally killed by wild gun-fire from the raiding police. What are we to make of a play in which the hero after his tragic death proceeds to jump up and sing:

> The bells of hell
> Go ting-a-ling-a-ling
> For you but not for me.
> Oh death where is thy
> Sting-a-ling-a-ling
> Or grave thy victory?[4]

How we understand this extraordinary event, how we manage it on the stage will determine how we approach the rest of the play, for it is the linch-pin of the play's structure.

Is Leslie's resurrection more than an audacious *coup de théâtre*, an irreverent thumbing of the nose at the audience, a discovery that for the last few moments they've been had, that the heart-breaking death, Teresa's moving farewell to her lover (so reminiscent of similar moments in Irish legend when those wild Irish queens mourn over their slain lover-princes[5]) was only theatre? Is Leslie testifying only to the tenacity of the theatre, how the actor always lives to act another day, that the only people who really die are those out there in the audience?

Certainly this is part of the moment's complex meaning. Music-hall is the operational principle behind the play's movement from the beginning. It is as though Pat were manager in his own theatre-saloon calling to centre stage the turns that are transformed into living plot—funny one moment, satiric the next, and heart shattering just before the grand finale. Everyone in the play, with the possible exception of the old Anglo-Irish patriot Monsewer, seems aware that he is on a stage as well as in the Dublin "brockel". The gaiety, irreverence, and riot counterpoint the dead seriousness of the crisis that engulfs them. As they all await news from Belfast that the I.R.A. boy has been executed, as they await whatever fate hangs over Leslie, they move from dramatic unit to unit employing theatrical techniques, punctuating their agony with song, dance, jokes, narratives, and improvisations. They move in and out of character and play their roles in fantastic guises. The debt to traditional music-hall entertainment and vaudeville is unmistakable and must be an essential metaphor in any production.

But, wonderful as it is for us to see the actor jump up from his pool of blood and declare that art and not death is his real business, that the intense, energised reality of the theatre guarantees the continuity of theatre in our lives if only we will attend and bear witness, there is also a mythic significance to Leslie's rebirth or rekindled life. It is difficult not to look on him as a *displacement* of the hero, the like of which inhabits not only Irish consciousness and legend, but also mythological patterns of the hero that all men recognise as part of their common spiritual-psychological freight. Leslie recalls the Exile, the Prince-Champion, the Sacrificial Lamb in twentieth-century scale and dress, helpless now, a nearly negative expression of the ancient formula.

As we watch the archetypal drama unfold, uncompromised by modern erosion, we can identify five stages or actions that go to make up the completed structure in which Lesie acts out his heroic role: *Prologos*—The World suffers and awaits the Hero; *Epiphany* —The Hero arrives and is glorified; *Agon*—He works to relieve suffering; *Pathos* with *Peripety*—He suffers betrayal and departs or is destroyed; and *Anagnorisis*—The Hero is reborn with a new promise.[6] This is the way *The Hostage* works. Act I is prologue with several divertissements ending in the *Epiphany*—the entrance of Leslie. Act II accelerates the pace and is the *Agon* in which is already operating the machinery of the *Pathos*-betrayal. On the hinge of Act II and III, Leslie's doom is sealed; the guilt-stricken entertain only abortive fantasies of rescue for him. And on the shank of Act III, Leslie dies and takes his special magic with him. Finally, in a kind of reprise of his initial appearance at the end of Act I, he returns in pentecostal triumph, declaring himself and bestowing his blessing, however meagre.

That any number of basic myths could fit into this pattern is obvious, but I am most struck by the way it recalls the Lohengrin legend, its events and even its cast of characters. The parallelism, direct and inverse, cannot be detailed here, but I should at least like to point to the fact that while it is the revelation of Lohengrin's name as *Lohengrin* at the Court of Brabant that exhausts his magic and ends his service there, for Leslie it is being known by the name of *Englishman* in Ireland that spells his doom—an interesting historical modulation.

This modulation reduces courtly splendor to modern squalor. Brought to Dublin as the hostage, Leslie is held captive in a whorehouse that is also a haven for the fugitive, down-and-out I.R.A. underground. The inhabitants of this house compose a microcosm of a world in upheaval and dislocation. It is a symbol

THE ART OF BRENDAN BEHAN

of Ireland—an unreality where politics, nationalism, religion, the military, the family, and love are grown sick. Love becomes prostitution; the military is madness; nationalism is crime. Religion becomes perversion, politics cowardice and nihilism. The family, in the ordinary sense, disappears. It exists only as grotesque parody. All the habitués of the "knocking shop" adopt familial relationships to Leslie and make him the object of their fantasy-life. Monsewer, symbolically Leslie's maternal uncle, sees in the boy his own "English" sacrifice for Ireland. Pat and Meg see their responsibility as surrogate parents to the orphan-exile but are incapable of rising to that responsibility. The whores, as sisters, want to seduce and mother him, but the efforts are only tentative and ultimately fail. Mr. Mulleady and the queers want Leslie for their own as a brother. It is they who turn informers and bring down the final absurdity on the life of the boy they try to save. Teresa, the sweetheart-"wife", wants her man alive and free to take her away as they planned together, but in the end, like Lohengrin's Elsa, she cannot order her resolve to accomplish her dreams.

Three Irelands struggle for dominance and recognition in the play. The Ireland of contemporary, illegal Republican fanaticism, dedicated to the final destruction of all things English in all of Ireland, is represented by the cowardly I.R.A. officers in charge of Leslie. Pat and Monsewer stand for the Ireland of glorious memory of the Troubles and Easter Week, needing no justification beyond the private experience of valor and sacrifice that they claim to remember. Then there is the Ireland that actually exists. In *The Hostage*, this nation belongs to the police, their sirens, rifle-fire, and terror. This Ireland seems to be good for informers to run to, nothing more.

Sex, liquor, fear, and bigotry demolish the integrity of the I.R.A. men. Self-delusion and disappointment bring down Pat and his national dream, and Monsewer is mad. Official Ireland is cursed with the task of mopping up her own dreaming children.

Behan seems to be saying, "See what has become of Ireland, of the world!" But the irony implicit in that final song, "The bells of hell", appears to be Leslie's unspoken, heroic declaration that, "Lo, I am with you always." And not just as an actor, but as whatever there is in life that is heroic and regenerative, that is, divine and indestructible. The business of this play is to salvage exhausted heroism, to revive the hero after destroying him, in order to prove

that the structure out of which he has emerged can itself be re-
newed and authenticated. The hero traditionally cannot be destroyed; he may be tortured, mutilated, and killed, but his essence
is imperishable, and it regenerates that life within its influence.
So in *The Hostage*, Leslie, as hero, survives every absurdity and
accident. He survives even history. By his sacrifice he becomes what
every man or woman in the symbolic brothel requires of him. He
may be the New Nation, the Son, the Brother, the Lover. . . .

In Behan's refusal to give his gallous Irish play a typical Irish
hero to ruin and later honor (the too-familiar pattern in Ireland),
by making him English, equipped with urban cynicism and un-
burdened of any of the conventional credences of nation, religion,
or culture, there is implied the notion that Irish parochial allegi-
ances can no longer be tolerated; the Irish world must be large
enough to accept Leslie. Monsewer's racism, once a battle-cry
against oppression, his definition of a race as a group of people
who have lived together for a long time won't work for the big
world any more. Behan suggests that his, Ireland's, and our sympathies must extend beyond the comfortable Irish-Celtic (or American) sentimentalities to a broader commitment and emotion. So,
Leslie is a British soldier whom the whores, pimps, patriots, and
whatever simply cannot hate as Irishmen conventionally hate Englishmen. They would everyone save Leslie if they could, but their
lives are so distorted and warped by clinging to the phantoms of
the past, their society so cruelly hung-up, that any effort to save
him is grotesque and abortive, or else there is no effort at all.

This world is illicit—a whorehouse where men play at illusion
and deception. The fine old Dublin house, now degraded, is analogous to a theatre, as Ireland herself is analogous to a theatre where
the native dramatic sensibility is active enough to make daily life
resemble a dramatic artifact (a condition that helps explain why
Ireland developed no formal, national drama until this century).
At any rate, *The Hostage* and Ireland, both, present a dynamic
confrontation between life and art, where the imagination provides
the spirit and goes a long way toward defining the form of experience. This intense imagination may, as Shaw held in *John Bull's
Other Island*, degrade Irish life; it may be a substitute for legitimate
experience and responsibility, but its dramatic artistic character is
unmistakable.

If then, Leslie's identification as a modern *displacement* of the traditional hero, scaled down by his unexceptional, under-privileged, working class Cockney background, is allowed, we should mark some of those signs in the play that point to his specialness and that hint at what in happier ages was heroism. Briefly, he has power to move hearts toward himself in genuine and significant ways; he places upon Teresa a complex role of loved one and Virgin Mary whom, on the evidence of Teresa's religious medal, he says she resembles. Through her he hopes to be saved. Teresa, like Ireland herself, proves incapable of saving anybody. The great Irish heroines before her were also unable to save their men from destruction, but they, at least, sacrificed them to a meaningful and usually worthy struggle that enhanced heroic values, not diminished them through absurd circumstance. Teresa's gentle love, as shown in her narrative of orphaned childhood, is nearly the limit of her contribution to a lost heroic dream. She describes how long ago she made of one desolate, little "mixed infant" a King of the May, implying that she can now make some kind of king of Leslie—if only in the restricted world of her imagination.

Still Leslie and Teresa each work significant transformations on the other. He reveals to her the breadth of the world and its experience, and she in turn brings him to an awareness of his situation regarding the I.R.A. Boy awaiting execution by the British in Belfast. Leslie learns for whom and what he is to die: for another boy very like himself, for a suffering nation, for souls in an earthly hell, and for love—his for the girl and the whorehouse-world's fleeting vision of love and purity in him. It is Leslie's vicarious death, a death with authentic, if remote, heroic resonance, that suddenly makes it clear to Teresa wherein Pat's pitiful failures lies: like the nation that bred and used him, he has lost the capacity for the heroic investment and can only stand helpless and dismayed by the ritual-death enacted before him. Her indictment is also her lament:

> Ah, it was not Belfast Jail or the six counties that was bothering you—but your lost youth and your crippled leg. I will never forget him. He died in a strange land and at home he has no one. I will never forget you, Leslie. Never, till the end of time.

Leslie, the orphan, the exile, the scapegoat, guileless, loved in a strange way by everyone, the one to whom everyone brings gifts,[7] the child-man, rallies those around him to try to reorganise their lives, and, if the results are disappointing and only bizarre, he has nevertheless provided them a glimpse of new possibilities for their defeated lives. In his prepossessing youth, his ingenuousness, and good cheer he seems almost to evoke the chivalrous epithet *debonair*.

A good deal of the play is given to teaching Leslie about Ireland and the British oppression—the story of Ireland's great suffering. But in contrast with the ultimate fact of Leslie's death, all that loses importance. His simplicity and ignorance, his love, his appeal to essential, humane impulse when at last he discovers the depth of his trouble, all point to a finer role and more generous purpose than might be suggested by such lapses into chauvinism and violence as erupt, for instance, out of his song at the end of the second act. In spite of such details of electric verisimilitude, Leslie works toward unity and reconciliation. His inarticulate cry is for simple justice, love, and life. His action is toward community. His ecstatic victory over death reminds us that, after all, even at our stupidest and most cruel, we can destroy only the body, and that we like Leslie, enjoy some mysterious continuity.

At the end, after the stanza of Pauline parody in his song, he sings about the possibility that we might have a shilling or two left over when the undertaker and insurance agent get through with us and urges us to spend it on a drink—a pint of Guinness, a eucharistic gesture. In a production of *The Hostage* at Franklin and Marshall College, Leslie at this moment tossed handfuls of dimes out into the audience; he offered to buy a drink for the dying, and the gesture was gratefully received.

The Hostage might be pushed in a different direction, toward the sardonic, toward an image of humiliation and defeat, or left in some dispiriting limbo, but that, I think, would go against the grain of the play. Behan's vitalism and energy, essentials of his artistic testimony, are affirmative, and affirmation of life's tenacity and will-to-love is the main thrust of this play. As in Behan's work as a whole, there is a spilling over of exuberance and compassion in *The Hostage* that can only be in praise of life.

When Leslie is brought captive to the whorehouse at the end of Act I, he sings and all join in:

There's no place on earth like the world.
There's no place wherever you be,

There's no place on earth like the world,
That's straight up and take it from me.

It's a simple faith and doesn't take us very far when compared
with older, grander schemes of hope; but for our abused and skepti-
cal times, it is remarkably like joy.

*　　*　　*

vi. *An Giall* and *The Hostage* Compared by *Richard Wall**

Recent events in Ireland have led to a revival of interest in
Brendan Behan's *Hostage*. The accidental topicality of the play
is reflected in the use of current newspaper headlines to advertise
a recent presentation of the play by Theatre Calgary, Alberta. Unfortunately, the only version of the play which is widely known,
the Joan Littlewood production of the late fifties when the I.R.A.
was something of a joke, is now in rather bad taste. The purpose
of this paper is to draw attention to *An Giall*,[8] the restrained and
almost forgotten tragi-comedy in Irish by Behan on which *The
Hostage*[9] is based.

Early in 1957, Gael-Linn, an Irish language revival organisation,
commissioned Behan to write a play for its Irish-speaking theatre.
On 16 June, 1958, *An Giall* (*The Hostage*) had its première in the
Damer Hall, Dublin. At the end of a successful run, Littlewood
offered to stage the play in London if Behan would translate it into
English. Behan accepted the offer and *The Hostage* was presented
to the English-speaking world by Theatre Workshop on 14 October
1958 at the Theatre Royal, Stratford, London. However, a comparison of the Irish and English texts reveals that *The Hostage*
is not a translation; it is a drastically modified version of the
original play.

The fact that *The Hostage* is more than a translation begins to
emerge as soon as one examines the characters in the two versions
of the play. There are ten characters in *An Giall*; there are fifteen
in *The Hostage*. The characters of *An Giall* are: Patrick, who runs
the establishment known as The Hole; Kate, his consort; Teresa,

---

* *Modern Drama*, XVIII (June 1975), 165–172.

the servant girl; Monsúr, the owner of The Hole; Leslie, the hostage; the I.R.A. Officer; the I.R.A. Volunteer; the Broy Harrier, a Special Branch detective; and two other I.R.A. volunteers. In *The Hostage* Pat's consort is named Meg and Kate is the name of an added character, the pianist. Teresa, Monsúr, Leslie, the Officer and Volunteer appear in *The Hostage*, but the Broy Harrier, who leads the raid on The Hole at the end of *An Giall*, undergoes something of a metamorphosis. His name has its origin in the popular nickname of the Special Branch detective force in Dublin Castle. The nickname is an ironic combination of the name of the founder of the force, Colonel Broy, and that of a cross-country running club, the Bray Harriers. Since all of this would probably be lost on an English audience, his name is changed and he appears in an expanded and largely comic role as the decaying civil servant, Mr. Mulleady, who reveals himself as a secret policeman during the raid on The Hole at the end of *The Hostage*. The two other I.R.A. volunteers, who appear briefly at the end of *An Giall*, are eliminated from *The Hostage*.

The effects of these changes are insignificant compared to the effects of the addition of seven characters to *The Hostage*: Rio Rita, homosexual navvy; Princess Grace, his coloured boyfriend; Miss Gilchrist, a social worker; two whores, Colette and Ropeen; the Russian Sailor; and Kate, the pianist. Colette and Ropeen are mentioned in *An Giall*, but they do not appear. The significance of Ropeen's name is lost in translation: the Irish word *rúipín* means little whore. The added characters contribute nothing to the plot of *The Hostage*, but they contribute a great deal to its tone, which is very different from that of the original. The function of the added characters can be seen by comparing the beginning of *The Hostage* with the beginning of *An Giall*. Before the curtain rises in *An Giall*, one hears the beating of drums and then the pipe lament, "Flowers of the Forest". The drums cease as the curtain rises, but the lament continues and is explained to Kate by Patrick. As the curtain rises in *The Hostage*, the added characters are dancing "a wild Irish jig" (p. 1). Pat and Meg sit and drink stout until it is over, and when the dancers leave she exclaims: "Thank God, that's over!" (p. 2). The tone of the opening of *An Giall* is solemn; the tone of the opening of *The Hostage* is that of a stage-Irish interlude, and such interludes interrupt the play with monotonous regularity.

The added characters also serve to make *The Hostage* a much more bawdy play than the original and allow the introduction of a host of topical English issues of the day, such as the Wolfenden Report on homosexual behaviour, immigration, race relations, the power of The Lord Chamberlain's Office, and even Brendan Behan himself. *An Giall* concentrates exclusively on Irish issues, such as Partition, the I.R.A. and its endless splits, the revival of Irish, romantic attitudes towards Irish history, and De Valera's remoteness from the people. These may be found in *The Hostage*, but they are almost buried under the avalanche of issues added for the amusement of an English audience.

There are no wild Irish jigs in *An Giall*. The only Irish dancing in the play is done by Teresa and Kate, who dance to a hornpipe which they hear on the radio at the end of the first act. As they dance to the beautiful and haunting Irish melody, "The Blackbird", they are interrupted by the appearance of Leslie. The melody is an oblique comment on Leslie: the Irish word for blackbird, *londubh*, is also a metaphor for hero. In *The Hostage* Teresa and Meg dance to a reel played by Kate on the piano. Gradually they are joined by everyone in the house in a swirling inter-weaving dance, which is interrupted by the appearance of Leslie. In both versions of the play dancers and hostage are abruptly juxtaposed, but the juxtaposition is more subtle and complex in the original.

Unlike *The Hostage*, there are very few songs in *An Giall*. In act one Patrick sings part of the refrain of the popular, patriotic ballad in Irish by Patrick Pearse, leader of the 1916 Rising: *"Oró! sé do bheatha 'bhaile!"* (p. 9). The greeting, "Hail! you are welcome home!" is an obvious ironic comment on the preparations for Leslie's reception. The song does not appear in *The Hostage*, probably because of the fact that it is never sung in English. However, the deletion is balanced by the addition of another song which, in the situation, is equally ironic. In act three, shortly before he is shot, Leslie sings, "When Irish Eyes are Smiling" (p. 93).

The most important difference between the songs of the two versions can be illustrated by comparing the openings of the third acts. When the curtain rises in *An Giall*, Leslie, who is alone on the stage, fitfully hums "God Save the Queen", "Rule Britannia" and "There'll always be an England" (p. 29). In *The Hostage*, Pat, who has an audience, seizes a bottle of stout and bursts into a wild song, which he also sings early in act one (pp. 5, 79). It celebrates an I.R.A. victory over the Black and Tans during the War of Independence. Such anti-English rebel songs, particularly the bitter "Who fears to speak of Easter Week" in act two (pp. 75–76), are a prominent feature of the play, but there are none in the original.

Pat's action of seizing a bottle of stout before bursting into song exemplifies one of the notable differences between the two versions. *The Hostage* has the dubious distinction of being one of the most drink-sodden plays in Anglo-Irish literature. As the directions for act one indicate, one of the main activities of the inhabitants of The Hole is the pursuit of stout. The ubiquitous drink in *An Giall*, tea, would probably appear most un-Irish to a non-Irish audience. There is only one reference to alcoholic drink in the play. In act three Patrick offers porter to the I.R.A. Officer and Volunteer, but the offer is bluntly refused.

It is very evident that a determined effort was made to make *The Hostage* more amusing and comprehensible to an English audience than the original. The hanging of the I.R.A. prisoner is discussed at the beginning of both. In *An Giall* Patrick states that there is no doubt that the boy will be hanged as high as *"Busáras"* (p. 1), the central bus depot in Dublin, which was the first tall, post-war building. In *The Hostage* *"Busáras"* becomes "Killymanjaro", which, Pat solemnly explains, is "a noted mountain off the south coast of Switzerland" (p. 3). There are many jokes in *The Hostage* which are not in the original. Some of them are very old and rather mechanically inserted:

> *Monsewer:* Those pipes, my boy, are the instrument of the ancient Irish race.
> *Soldier:* Permission to ask another question, sir.
> *Pat:* One step forward, march.
> *Soldier:* What actually is a race, guv?
> *Monsewer:* A race occurs when a lot of people live in one place for a long period of time.
> *Soldier:* I reckon our old sergeant-major must be a race; he's been stuck in that same depot for about forty years. (p. 61)

Behan appears to have adapted this exchange from the "Cyclops" episode of *Ulysses* in which Leopold Bloom is twitted for his definition of a nation: "the same people living in the same place."[10] Ned Lambert laughingly responds: "By God, then, . . . if that's so

I'm a nation for I'm living in the same place for the past five years."
Perhaps the stalest joke in the play is Pat's definition of an Anglo-
Irishman in act one: "A Protestant with a horse" (p. 15).

Much of the wit of *An Giall* is not present in *The Hostage*,
simply because it is not translatable. The Gaelic League is mocked
in *An Giall* as Patrick explains to Kate that it was the Anglo-Irish
Treaty of 1921 which unbalanced Monsúr. The mockery is made
possible by the fact that the Irish word *conradh* means treaty and
league:

> *Kate:* What drove him out of his mind . . .?
> *Patrick:* The Treaty.
> *Kate:* The League? What League? The Gaelic League? Yearra,
> that crowd would drive anybody out of his mind. (p. 5)

There is a fine irony in Behan's use of the subtleties of Irish to
mock the Irish language revival organisation under whose auspices
his play was written and published.

There are a few Irish phrases in *The Hostage* to give it an Irish
flavour. One, which does not appear in *An Giall*, was obviously inserted because of what it suggests to English ears. It is Monsewer's
response to Leslie's description of his sergeant-major quoted above:
"Focail, Focaileile uait" (p. 61). The phrase, which means "Word,
another word from you," makes little if any sense in the context
in which it appears. *The Hostage* contains most of the conventional
expletives including that *sine qua non* of Dublin speech, "Jaysus"
(p. 29). There is no profanity in *An Giall*, though there is some
rather blunt language, such as Leslie's factual observation: "We're
nothing but a pair of bastards" (p. 25). Teresa is shocked and
bursts into tears. If the observation had been made by Leslie in
The Hostage, she might have been annoyed, but that is all, because
she swears and uses the word bastards herself (pp. 29, 57).

The effects of some changes are incongruous. At the beginning
of *An Giall*, Patrick informs Kate that the I.R.A. intends to turn
The Hole into a "Glass House", which, he explains, is "a sort of
Arbour Hill of their own" (p. 3). Since Patrick has been interned
in Arbour Hill and it is unlikely that any Irish adult does not know
its significance in modern Irish history, his choice of name is perfectly natural. In *The Hostage* Pat explains to Meg that Monsewer
wants to turn the place into "A kind of private Shepton Mallet of
his own" (p. 7). Since the significance of Arbour Hill is perfectly

clear from the context, the substitution of an English place for an Irish one is as unnecessary as it is incongruous. Minor changes of this nature, such as the substitution of "speak-easy" (*H*, p. 4) for "shebeen" (*G*, p. 1) abound. Perhaps the most incongruous change is in Teresa's explanation of her career. In *An Giall*, as Patrick questions her, she angrily rejects the suggestion that she lost her first job because she "stole something" (p. 13). In *The Hostage* Meg is the interrogator:

> *Meg:* Why did you leave there? Did you half-inch something?
> *Teresa:* What did you say?
> *Meg:* Did you half-inch something?
> *Teresa:* I never stole anything in my whole life. (p.39)

The use of Cockney rhyming slang by a Dublin whore is strange to say the least, but stranger still is the fact that a teenage convent girl from Ballymahon understands it.

The general attitude of the Irish towards Leslie, and the English in general, is much more hostile in *The Hostage* than in the original and it is reflected in their treatment of him. He first appears in *An Giall* as he walks happily into the room in which Teresa and Kate are dancing at the end of act one. He is followed by the I.R.A. Officer and Volunteer, who have their right hands in their pockets. In *The Hostage* he is blindfolded and pushed through the dancing mob by the two I.R.A. men. In both plays he asks the dancers not to stop, because he likes dancing. The curtain falls at this point in *An Giall*, but in *The Hostage* the I.R.A. Officer orders: "Keep your mouth shut, and get up there" (p. 41). The Officer allows Teresa to give Leslie a packet of cigarettes in *An Giall* (p. 20), but in *The Hostage* he confiscates it (pp. 48, 56). In act two of *An Giall* Kate apologises to Leslie when he overhears her brief, anti-English outburst, but in *The Hostage* Meg directs a lengthy, anti-English diatribe at Leslie. Kate's outburst is three sentences long (p. 21); Meg's diatribe in prose and song fills two pages (pp. 74–75). In *An Giall* Patrick is consistently paternal in his attitude to Leslie. This is most evident as he reassures Leslie at the opening of act three:

> *Patrick:* Well, Leslie.
> *Leslie:* Are you going to take me out to be shot now?
> *Patrick:* No, me son, no, nobody is going to take you out anyplace. (p. 28)

Pat's attitude in *The Hostage* is very different. He even holds Leslie responsible for Queen Victoria's alleged behaviour during the Famine:

> *Soldier:* What have I ever done to you that you should shoot me?
>
> *Pat:* I'll tell you what you've done. Some time ago there was a famine in this country and people were dying all over the place. Well, your Queen Victoria, or whatever her bloody name was, sent five pounds to the famine fund and at the same time she sent five pounds to the Battersea Dogs' Home so that no one could accuse her of having rebel sympathies. (p. 87)

Even the minor characters in *The Hostage* display hostility to Leslie. Rio Rita calls him a "murdering bastard" (p. 52) and suggests that he go back to his own country, as if he had some choice in the matter. Their covert hostility is suggested at the end of act two, when Leslie pleads with the mob surrounding him: "Surely one of you would let me go?" (p. 78). Instead of answering, they slink away leaving him alone in the room.

Consistent with the more hostile attitude of the Irish towards Leslie in *The Hostage*, the circumstances surrounding his death are very suspicious compared to those in the original. There is a large press in the room in which Leslie is kept in *An Giall*. In act one Monsúr prevents Patrick from removing it, because it might be useful as "a kind of refuge . . . for anyone staying in the room" (p. 15). Ironically, Leslie dies in this refuge. During the police raid, he is hurriedly bound, gagged and hidden by his captors in the press. By the time the raid is over and they can remove him, he is dead of suffocation. There is no doubt that his death is accidental. The press does not appear in *The Hostage*. Leslie is shot dead as he attempts to make a run for it during the police raid. It is not clear whether he is shot accidentally or deliberately, by the I.R.A. or by the police. However, since Monsewer threatens to shoot Leslie if the police come in, one is left with the strong suspicion that he is deliberately shot by the I.R.A.

The most striking feature of *An Giall* is the contrast between the innocent romance of Teresa and Leslie and the brutal world in which it takes place. The setting may be a bawdy house, but their behaviour is remarkably chaste. For a while they manage to transform the brothel room into a haven of innocence and beauty, but

144

the audience is not allowed to forget the menace outside. Whenever Teresa enters and leaves, she does not open and close the door herself; it is done for her by the I.R.A. guards lurking outside. There is far less emphasis on the romance in *The Hostage* and its tone is altered. Leslie and Teresa are alone on the stage for about three quarters of act two of *An Giall*; this is reduced to about one-third in *The Hostage*. They are both eighteen years of age in *An Giall*, and Leslie, who is an innocent from Lancashire, is about seven months older than Teresa. In *The Hostage* they are older, tougher and obviously more experienced sexually: both are nineteen, but now Teresa is about seven months older than Leslie, who is a tough Cockney. In *An Giall* Teresa is described as being "neat" and "pretty" (p. 8); in *The Hostage* she is "a strong hefty country girl" (p. 27), and she shows little hesitation in hopping into bed in response to Leslie's blunt invitation.

The reasons for the differences between the two versions of the play are fairly obvious. A serious play about the age-old "Irish Question" stood little chance of notice in England in the late fifties, particularly in view of the fact that it contains no drinking except tea, no wild Irish jigs, no anti-English rebel songs and no mob scenes. By the random addition of such ingredients, *The Hostage* panders to popular conceptions of the Irish. *An Giall* contains many allusions to Irish figures, organisations and places which would probably be lost on English audiences. This problem is handled in *The Hostage* by substituting English allusions for many of the Irish ones, but the effects are frequently incongruous. The appeal of *The Hostage* is widened by making it bawdy and peppering it with allusions to most of the popular issues of the day, ranging from the Wolfenden Report to nuclear disarmament, none of which appear in the original.

The principal effects of the changes are the destruction of the integrity of the original play, a drastic alteration of its tone, and a reduction of the impact of its most striking feature: the tender romance between Teresa, the Irish orphan girl, and Leslie, the English orphan boy, in a brutal world that will not permit their simple unconscious and human solution to the eight centuries of hatred and bloodshed which have divided their people.

It is clear from Ulick O'Connor's exploration of the Behan-Littlewood collaboration that it would be very difficult if not impossible to determine who is responsible for specific differences between the two versions of the play.[11] For example, Behan obviously provided the phrase *"Focail, Focaileile uait"*, but did the idea to insert such a phrase in *The Hostage* come from him, her or one of the actors? Behan does not appear to have cared about such matters, because he approved of the results of the collaboration. In *Brendan Behan's Island* he writes:

> I saw the rehearsals of this version [*An Giall*] and while I admire the producer, Frank Dermody, tremendously, his idea of a play is not my idea of a play. I don't say that his is inferior to mine or that mine is inferior to his—it just so happens that I don't agree with him. He's of the school of Abbey Theatre naturalism of which I'm not a pupil. Joan Littlewood, I found, suited my requirements exactly. She has the same views on the theatre that I have, which is that the music hall is the thing to aim at for to amuse people and any time they get bored, divert them with a song or a dance. I've always thought T. S. Eliot wasn't far wrong when he said that the main problem of the dramatist today was to keep his audience amused; and that while they were laughing their heads off, you could be up to any bloody thing behind their backs; and it was what you were doing behind their bloody backs that made your play great.[12]

However, there is circumstantial evidence that Behan's response to the results of his collaboration with Joan Littlewood was not always so enthusiastic. His brother Brian describes an incident which happened one night during the first run of *The Hostage*. Behan turned round suddenly to Brian in the packed theatre and said, "Fuck Joan Littlewood."[13]

* * *

vii. Hostages to History: Title as Dramatic Metaphor in
The Hostage by *Paul M. Levitt**

The breezy, madcap surface action of *The Hostage* masks a serious and poignant attack on Irish devotion to the past: that is, to the historical dream of uniting Ireland—north and south—and driving out the British. Although the title of the play refers to the

* *Die Neueren Sprachen* (Frankfurt), XXIV (October 1975), 401–406.

young English soldier taken prisoner by the I.R.A., the title also serves as a dramatic metaphor to implicate the mad devotion to an empty dream which makes hostages out of others in the play.

Brendan Behan's *The Hostage* is a frenetic play, difficult to sum up and easy to distort, and it has mostly been reviewed favorably rather than well. There is about it an effortless air of madcap fun, which at first reading is rather deceptive. Because of the frolicking atmosphere of jigs and reels, set in the midst of apparently un-connected scenes, the play appears to be a kind of light variety show or vaudeville. However, the riotous nature of the work has obscured its underlying seriousness. Behan once remarked that "the first duty of a writer is to let his country down. He knows his own people the best. He has a special responsibility to let them down".[14] A believer in the subversive principle in human affairs, Behan, rather than reinforce Irish devotion to Ireland, examines and reveals the debilitating nature of their senseless idealism. In *The Hostage*, which opened in its revised form,[15] before an English audience, 11 July 1959, at Wyndham's theatre, London, Behan attacks the traditional Irish dependence on the past.

The title of the play has several meanings and provides a key to understanding Behan's attitude toward tradition and, in particular, the relation of past to present. The title, *The Hostage*, ostensibly refers to Leslie Williams, the young English soldier who has been taken prisoner by the Irish Republican Army (I.R.A.). There is no particular reason for the choice of Leslie as a prisoner; he is selected as the hostage simply because he is an Englishman (ironically, a National Serviceman), and because he happens to be walking out of a dance when members of the I.R.A. are looking for a hostage. It is this accidental combination of events that leads to the eighteen-year-old boy's death, and to his becoming, in a loose I.R.A. manner of speaking, a sacrifice for the "cause".

In general, there are two reasons for taking a hostage. First, a hostage may serve as a means for an injured party or group to avenge itself by injuring another. Second, a hostage may be used for purposes of negotiation. The hostage serves to persuade the opposing force to discontinue its present course of action, *if* the opposing force wishes the safe return of the hostage. In the play the first reason is germane, the second is not. A newspaper article reports that "If [the boy who is being held in the Belfast Jail for I.R.A. activities is] executed—the I.R.A. declare that Private Leslie Alan Williams will be shot as a reprisal" (p. 78). The English government, however, is indifferent to what happens to Leslie Williams, a fact which is not lost on Leslie. Hence, when Meg tries to comfort him by reminding him of the possibility of a reprieve being granted to the boy in the Belfast Jail, Leslie replies bitterly:

> You're as barmy as him if you think that what's happening to me is upsetting the British Government. I suppose you think they're all sitting round in their West End clubs with handkerchiefs over their eyes, dropping tears into their double whiskies. Yeah, I can just see the Secretary of State for War now waking up his missus in the night: "Oh Isabel-Cynthia love, I can hardly get a wink of sleep wondering what's happening to that poor bleeder Williams."
>
> (p. 89)

He knows that his death is near at hand. The reason for his being executed is the fanaticism and the desire for vengeance on the part of the I.R.A. Leslie is a victim of history and patriotism, of romance and nationalism; he is a victim of the I.R.A. dream to unite Ireland —north and south—and drive the British out. In other words, Leslie is a hostage to those who are victims of an historical obsession.

But Leslie is not alone in being affected by the past. A good many of the characters in the play are still fighting the old war. The setting of the action is a brothel, owned by Monsewer, a former general in the Irish Republican Army, and run by Pat, a soldier who served under the general's command. Monsewer was raised in England, but upon learning that his mother was Irish became passionately Irish. The absurdity of Monsewer's romantic fervour is progressively disclosed throughout the play. We learn, for example, that when he first arrived in Ireland, he refused to speak anything but Gaelic; however, since the typical Irishman understands only English, the zealous convert had to be accompanied on trams and buses by an interpreter, so that the driver would know where to let him off.

Monsewer's brothel is another example of the way he romanticizes the past. Pat says of the brothel:

> *Pat:* Monsewer doesn't know anything about these matters.
> *Meg:* Course he does, Pat.

Pat: He doesn't.

Meg: He must know.

Pat: No. He thinks everybody in this house are gaels, patriots or Republicans on the run. (pp. 10–11)

Monsewer stubbornly maintains his illusions of past glory in the present atmosphere of debauchery and deterioration.

The brothel can be read as a metaphorical comment on the value of the old cause in the present. Consider for a moment: a man will go to a brothel to escape present misery. Love with a prostitute is a temporary game of make-believe, played for a fee, and the satisfaction received depends on one's ability to forget himself in a moment of illusion. Similarly, the old cause of the I.R.A. is a romantic illusion, dependent on a fanatical belief in the past and a blindness to the reality of the present. In the brothel, the unhappy realities of the present are softened by the dreams of an idealised past. Meg, for example, feels insulted when Pat alludes to her being a whore; she haughtily maintains her dignity by insisting that she is a "true patriot" (p. 19), and demands that she be recognised as such.

Pat, on the other hand, tells us that he deserted the cause when he realised that the I.R.A. were more interested in politics than in domestic social issues.

> You wouldn't recall, I suppose, the time in County Kerry when the agricultural labourers took over five thousand acres of land from Lord Tralee? . . . 1925 it was, They had it all divided fair and square and were ploughing and planting in great style. I.R.A. H.Q. sent down orders that they were to get off the land. That social question would be settled when we'd won the thirty-two-county republic. . . . The Kerry men said they weren't greedy, they didn't want the whole thirty-two counties, their own five thousand acres would do 'em for a start. . . . I agreed with them. I stayed there and trained a unit. By the time I'd finished we could take on the I.R.A., the Free State Army, or the British bloody Navy, if it came to it. (pp. 32–33)

The abstraction, the "cause"—the reunification of Ireland, north and south—is more important than the cultivation of five thousand acres. It was just such fanaticism that provoked Sean O'Casey's contempt for the I.R.A. No wonder then that Pat's disillusionment is reminiscent of Juno's impatience with her son's mindless insistence, in *Juno and the Paycock*, that "a principle's a principle".

Pat is clearly the most complex and interesting character in the play; metaphorically, he is the hostage of the title and the hero of the play. He embodies the intellectual and emotional struggle of present day Ireland; he is torn between the romance of the past and the reality of the present. At one point he says,

> This is nineteen-sixty, and the days of the heroes are over this forty years past. Long over, finished and done with. The I.R.A. and the War of Independence are as dead as the Charleston.
> (p. 3)

but at another point,

> Are you aware, Miss Gilchrist, that you are speaking to a man who was a commandant at the times of the troubles.   (p. 80)

Intellectually, Pat is able to distinguish between the illusions of the past and the facts of the present, and is able sensibly to evaluate the significance of the cause. But emotionally, he claims a share in the patriotic glamour of the past.

What Pat has become—because of his ambivalence—is rudely expressed by Meg when she says to him:

> . . . the day you gave up work to run this house for Monsewer and take in the likes of this lot, you became a butler, a Republican butler, a half-red footman—a Sinn Fein skivvy.   (p. 84)

In general, Meg is accusing Pat of using "The Troubles" as an excuse to rationalise his present sloth and dishonesty. Therein lies the problem. If Pat is to keep a semblance of self-respect, he must maintain both the worth of the old cause—the struggle for independence—*and* the charade that Monsewer's house is not a brothel, but rather a hideout for I.R.A. gunmen on the run. The two attitudes, of course, are incompatible. The old cause was indeed a worthy cause; but the war is over. To pretend that the war is still being fought creates a situation in which people feel obliged to iterate their past deeds and apologise for their present indifference. Hence the dilemma of present day Ireland: how to get on with the affairs of the day when so many I.R.A. fanatics are still observing the old arguments and are still fighting the old war. Pat sums up the problem when he says:

Pat: Do you know what the worst thing is [about being in prison for I.R.A. activities]?
Officer: No.
Pat: The other Irish patriots in along with you.

The Officer, a 1960s I.R.A. fanatic, is insulted and ironically gives point to Pat's observation when he says:

Officer: What did you say?
Pat: Your fellow patriots, in along with you. There'd be a split straight away.
Officer: If I didn't know you were out in 1916 ...   (p.51)

The Officer is, in fact, the most frightening example in the play of unquestioning devotion to the past. He has no sympathy for Leslie's plight and carries out his assignment with prim seriousness that often borders on the grotesque. He speaks in short, terse sentences, and fastidiously refuses to deviate from the business at hand. When Leslie mentions his attraction to Teresa, the Officer ignores him; when Pat attempts a joke, the Officer's response is: "Can we be serious, please?" (p. 31). The Officer is an automaton, programmed with a single-minded conviction: that the I.R.A. is right. He sees things in terms of simple absolutes. If a man fought for the I.R.A. in 1916, *ipso facto* he is a good man; his present activities are irrelevant. He considers himself a moral man and is offended that the I.R.A. must rendezvous in a brothel. He is willing to allow the plans for Leslie's execution to proceed without objection, but he is reluctant to allow Meg entry to the boy's room.

Officer: I don't think we should. He's in our care and we're morally responsible for his spiritual welfare. ... Jesus, Mary and Joseph, but it would be a terrible thing for him to die with a sin of impurity on his—   (p.73)

The devout Officer sees no inconsistency in his attitudes.

Significantly, both Leslie and Teresa are orphans—and thus symbolically free from allegiance to the past. For this reason, they are the only characters in the play who dream of a future.

Leslie: ... If I get away will you come and see me in Armagh?
Teresa: I will, Leslie.
Leslie: I want all the blokes in the billet to see you. They all got pictures on the walls. Well, I never had any pictures, but now

151

I've got you. Then we could have a bloody good time in Belfast
together.
    Teresa: It would be lovely, ashore.
    Leslie: I'm due for a week-end's leave an' all . . .
    Teresa: I could pay my own way, too.
    Leslie: No, you needn't do that. I've got enough for both of
us . . .   (pp. 101–102)

In the midst of the depravity of the brothel, the two orphans make
love and plan to see each other again. The act of love, which is
literally and figuratively at the centre of the play, can be read as
Behan's comment on the possibility of transcending the past by
means of love. Teresa, a convent-trained girl, willingly accepts
Leslie, a Protestant, English soldier. Two people who, in the context of English-Irish relations, would normally be irreconcilable
are, in fact, not, because they have neither an historical sense of
past injury nor a present desire to maintain old arguments. It
would seem, then, that Behan is saying that if we can dissociate
ourselves from the past—become orphans, as it were—we might
have some chance of getting on together and, consequently, settling
our differences.

The point should not be lost on us that it is Teresa—the Irish
girl—who asks Leslie about England's historical cruelties to Ireland, and that Leslie's reply constitutes for both of them, by the
end of the play, an accurate statement of their feelings.

    Teresa: Anyway, he [Monsewer] left your lot and came over
here and fought for Ireland.
    Leslie: Why, was somebody doing something to Ireland?
    Teresa: Wasn't England, for hundreds of years?
    Leslie: That was donkey's years ago. Everybody was doing
something to someone in those days.   (pp. 57–58)

Leslie is interested in good times, in having a girl friend whom he
can love and whose photograph he can proudly show to his friends;
he has no interest in, and probably even less comprehension of, a
life based on perpetual bitterness because of an historic feud.

However, for the I.R.A. war is a game. Forty years after 1916,
the war of independence has degenerated into a romantic and
vaguely dangerous pastime that permits grown men to meet
clandestinely and go on raids, stand guard duty, and talk bravely
about being at war.

> *Leslie:* Does it really mean they're going to shoot me?
> *Mulleady:* I'm afraid so.
> *Leslie:* Why?
> *Monsewer:* You are the hostage.
> *Leslie:* But I ain't done nothing.
> *Officer:* This is war. (p. 78)

"You are the hostage" is the kind of language children use when they choose sides to play war games and "cops and robbers". But in the brothel the game is for real. According to the rules, if the English execute the boy in Belfast Jail, the I.R.A. will execute Leslie Williams. Leslie's pathetic plaint, "But I ain't done nothing", sums up the problem of engaging in guerilla warfare during peacetime: it is mainly the innocent who suffer. True to form, the Officer dismisses Leslie's plea with the statement, "This is war".

Unfortunately for the two orphans, they are surrounded by the past and cannot escape its murderous effects. The idea of encirclement is to be found throughout the play, providing an apt metaphor of history as a prison. The young are entrapped by their elders. In fact, Leslie is forced to stand within a circle drawn on the floor. When Leslie is shot, attempting to escape the circle and free himself, the dramatic metaphor is complete. The hostage Leslie Williams is, in effect, executed in reprisal for the death of the boy in Belfast Jail. The war between England and Ireland goes on. The circle is unbroken. That Leslie dies accidentally is important, because his death suggests not only the carelessness in thought and deed of the I.R.A. fanatics, but also the danger of pretense. In this latter regard it is instructive to look at Pat. He is the moral touchstone in the play. He is literally a "good" man fallen among thieves; and we wait and watch to see what he will do . When he apologies for Leslie's death on the grounds that it was unintentional, and then proceeds implicitly to defend what has happened, we know the price of pretense.

> *Pat:* Don't cry, Teresa. It's no one's fault. Nobody meant to kill him.
> *Teresa:* But he's dead.
> *Pat:* So is the boy in Belfast Jail. (p. 108)

We become what we pretend to be. Surrounded (the encirclement idea again) by narrow-minded patriots, degenerates, and impractical dreamers, Pat becomes one of them. By pretending that he and the others are hostage-bound to the old cause, until such time as Ireland, north and south, is united, Pat unwittingly contributes to the death of Leslie. The point is clear. By condoning madness, Pat, the "good" man, is largely responsible for what happens to Teresa and Leslie, innocent lovers like Romeo and Juliet, who, victimised by an irrational and romantic pride in a heritage of calamitous fighting, are, finally, sacrificed to a past they neither care about nor understand.

NOTES

1 The other play reviewed is *The Iron Harp*, by Michael O'Riordan.

2 Two editions of the play are available, and each should be consulted. Grove Press includes *The Hostage* with *The Quare Fellow* in its Evergreen Black Cat series, BC79 (1964). This text is spare of stage directions and differs in other interesting respects from the out-of-print edition published by Methuen and Co., London (1958, revised and reprinted until 1964). The Methuen edition is richer in detail, but neither edition contains tunes for the songs. This and subsequent notes are the author's.

3 Ludwick Flaszen, "After the Avant-garde", *The Theatre in Poland*, X (July-August 1968), 13.

4 Quotations from the play in this paper are taken from the Grove Press edition. It is interesting to observe how Littlewood and her troop used this same song to quite different purposes in their next international success, *Oh, What a Lovely War!* In the context of that script, the song is altogether bitter and sardonic as doughboys bury their dead knowing that they will be next and dead forever.

5 Deirdre is perhaps the best example of the type, and Teresa's closing speech clearly echoes Deirdre's lament for the slain Naisi. See W. B. Yeats's and J. M. Synge's Deirdre plays.

6 I am using *Agon*, *Pathos*, and *Anagnorisis* after Northrop Frye. See *Anatomy of Criticism* (Princeton, 1957), p. 192. There is also a suggestion of what Frye identifies as *Sparagmos* in the disorganisation and violence of the play's finale.

7 In the Methuen edition, the stage direction at the beginning of Act II reads: "The house appears to be still, but in the dark corners and doorways, behind the piano and under the stairs, people are hiding, waiting for an opportunity to contact the prisoner, to see what he looks like and to take him comforts like cups of tea, bible tracts, cigarettes and stout."

8 Breandán Ó Beacháin, *An Giall* (Baile Átha Cliath, n.d., An Chomhairle Náisiúnta Drámaíochta). All quotations are from this edition and the translations are mine.

9 Brendan Behan, *The Hostage* (London, 1962). All quotations are from this the third edition of the play. *The Hostage* was first presented by Theatre Workshop on 14 October, 1958 at the Theatre Royal, Stratford, London. A revised version of the play was presented by Theatre Workshop at the Théâtre des Nations Festival in Paris on 3 April, 1959, and again, with further revisions, at Wyndham's Theatre on 11 June, 1959. The differences between the three versions of the play are not material to this discussion.

10 James Joyce, *Ulysses* (New York), (1961), p. 331.

11 Ulick O'Connor, *Brendan Behan* (London, 1970), pp. 195–208.

12 Brendan Behan, *Brendan Behan's Island* (London, 1962), p. 17.

13 O'Connor, p. 207.

14 As quoted in: Hatch, R.: "The Critic's View: The Roaring Presence of Brendan Behan." *Horizon* III: 3 (January, 1961), 113. This and subsequent note are the author's.

15 All references in the text to *The Hostage* are from the third edition, revised, 1962, printed in London by Methuen & Co. Ltd. Also, in the text instead of using for quotations the heading "Soldier", I have substituted his name: Leslie (Williams).

8

Brendan Behan's Island

i. The Two Faces of Ireland by *Louis MacNeice**

The more the Irish pour out of Ireland the more books pour out of it too. These two latest autobiographical pieces[1] complement each other very nicely and Paul Hogarth's illustrations to Brendan Behan's book add a strong dose of atmosphere; you can almost smell these pencil drawings of pubs and peasants and slum children and bogs and curraghs and graveyards.

As for Behan's text, any one who has read his very vivid *Borstal Boy* will know what to expect: he writes like a good talker talking, with plenty of hyperbole and emphasis; this is a book who drinks may read. It is of course somewhat thrown together: when he has nothing particular to say he will put in a traditional ballad or the whole of "The Groves of Blarney". His own writing shows humanity, gusto, and a formidable wit, as when he is talking about the new social climbers of Dublin:

> It started off with top-hats and white ties and getting into the gentry and then to chatting about the servant problem with the Anglo-Irish Horse-Protestants (who at least were reared to it) and it went from that to late dinner and now it's Angst, no less.

The best thing in this book is "The Confirmation Suit", which, though a remembered episode, reads like a good short story. Behan in fact is much better at narrative than at exposition. Some of his comments on Ireland, however, are much to the point, as when in a chapter entitled "The Black North" he writes:

> I won't say that there's no difference between people north and south of the border, but I will say, without fear of contradiction, that there's less difference between them than there is between, say, a Yorkshireman and a Somerset man.

* The *Observer* (London), (30 September 1962), p. 29.

I once expressed exactly this opinion in a pamphlet for the British Council and had a blue pencil put through it. Behan himself has far more in common with a Belfast writer like Sam Thompson than either of them has with any English writer. Many people in the north, however, will find him unduly irreverent about the Orange processions:

> It's a colourful show, I must admit, and I think when the country is again united, we'll keep it going under the auspices of the Tourist Board—after all, people travel to distant countries to see these tribal ceremonies and dances and, as those up here in the North are as good as any to be found, we might as well make a bit of money out of them.

It is a pity that Paul Hogarth did not draw one of these processions.

* * *

ii. Pen and Gab by *Anon**

Good talk is endemic in Ireland. A poor man will regale you with talk better than his more prosperous neighbour, for poverty does not make him insensitive to language or blind to the world around him. Mr. Behan is proud to come from the Dublin working-class; good talk is his birthright, and being a poet and a natural writer he transcribes his talk into the most readable English.

He suggests that he is just setting down an evening's talk over the drinks. Certainly his book is inconsequential enough, and gives a much less complete survey of "his island" than Paul Hogarth's sensitive pencil drawings. Mr. Hogarth records that difference of atmosphere which strikes the visitor to Ireland more forcibly than the native. He is equally successful in depicting slum children and townspeople, particularly old women, as with the mountains and coasts of the west. Mr. Behan is inclined to play down differences: "Such as exist between Britain and Ireland", he says,

> are due more to economic and social environment than to racial characteristics. If you go into a pub in Manchester, Belfast, Dublin, Liverpool, or London you will hear people sing the same

* The *Times Literary Supplement* (London), (12 October 1962), p. 791.

> song. . . . My sister lives in a new town in Sussex and is more interested in the problems of the woman next door than in the differences between the English and the Irish.

Belfast and Dublin interest him almost equally, and he writes more observantly about Belfast than about Dublin, where he chiefly talks about himself. For he tells us a great deal about himself, either directly that he was in the I.R.A. and that he is a socialist, or indirectly that he is an Irish-speaker and the friend of poets and artists, that he is a generous and tender-hearted man who has lived among toughs and sportsmen, that he is arrogantly anti-clerical though a Roman Catholic. His understanding of Irish affairs is shrewd, but his knowledge of Ireland seems limited to the towns and the Irish-speaking districts of the west. He feels at home among the working-class people of Dublin, "they're the only real people here"; and of Belfast he says:

> The rural parts of the North are very beautiful, but being a city man myself I prefer Belfast to the country outside it. Partly the reason for my fondness for it is that it is the heart of proletarian Ireland.

Looking at Irish life from this angle he sees

> the great sameness of depression in all Irish cities . . . exactly the same amount of porridge is doled out to the workers whether the government is a Dublin or a Belfast one.

This political nihilism lets him understand only a very small section of his fellow countrymen. He loves the racy life of the poor in city slums or Atlantic islands, and he mocks the empty life of the "horse-protestants—horse-faced ladies and stout, red-faced men, the next best thing to animals". He cares nothing for the skill and learning of the professional classes, "Catholics as well as Protestants, lawyers as well as doctors", seeing them all as snobs and Unionists at heart.

> I don't know many working writers in Ireland, because there aren't many. There are civil servants, spoiled priests, judges, ex-convicts, retired nuns, and escaped agriculturalists who write . . .

but his satire as he warms to it becomes merely silly.

It is not for his political opinions, however, that one listens gladly to Mr. Behan, but for his fund of good anecdotes, whether they briefly record a witty repartee or build up an elaborate tale such as his grandmother's encounter with the tinkers or his own adventure with the doped greyhound. When he is short of such tales he recites a stirring ballad, and from Belfast for good measure provides both an Orange and a rebel ballad. Such old familiars as "The Groves of Blarney", and other verses from the 'Protestant culture" which he affects to despise, fill up more pages than they deserve, and his chapter on the Aran Islands is padded out with a long folk-tale on the usual "tinder-box" theme. The modern verses that he quotes, including some fine poems of his own in Irish and English, are much fresher and more welcome. Best of all are two short stories in which he catches exactly the rhythm and vocabulary of Dublin talk: "A Woman of no Standing" is a restrained though bitter anti-clerical sketch, but "The Confirmation Suit" is a deliciously comic and tender reminiscence of childhood.

* * *

iii. Streets Broad and Narrow by *Michael Campbell**

If this book were by a writer of no repute, one would describe it briefly as a patchwork of funny stories, patriotic ballads, potted history and guidebook information, very little of it being either new to students of Ireland or presented with literary art, and the whole of it being decked out with an enormous quantity of sketchbook drawings by Paul Hogarth. There are almost eighty, and no fewer than sixty of them take up a full page and are exhibited on special yellow paper. They do evoke Ireland, but any drawings of toothless faces in Irish pubs and of Irish shopfronts with "O'Brien" and "McGrath" on them will do this; and I can see no especial originality in these rather spidery sketches.

But, since this book is by Brendan Behan, a writer of international repute, it seems to demand a more thorough review, in spite of its modest subtitle.

It largely consists of Four Parts concerning Dublin, the South, the West, and the North.

The funny stories are good ones, provided you are open to the

* *Saturday Review* (New York), XLV (3 November 1962), 48.

charm of Irish hypocrisy, intoxication, and ignorance. I am, but only just.

The patriotic ballads are usually printed in full, and you have to be very much of a mind that is charmed by "O Ireland, mother Ireland, you love them still the best."

The history mainly concerns the Troubles, the murder of Michael Collins, the signing of the Treaty—surely terribly familiar stuff. ("It all resulted in the division of Ireland in 1920, under the leadership of a Dublin Unionist named Carson and a Northerner named Craig, later Lord Craigavon".)

The guidebook information one can hardly believe comes from the pen of Mr. Behan at all. This, for instance:

> Most of the Guinnesses live around Castleknock which is just on the far side of the Phoenix Park. This is one of the largest national parks in Europe. If you could imagine all the parks in Central London—from Kensington Gardens up to Hampstead Heath—put together, you'd have some idea of its size. It is less than two miles from the centre of the city and is very popular both in winter and summer.

Interspersed among these Four Parts, which are really talking parts, are interval entertainments. These are taken chiefly from Mr. Behan's past writings, and they are superior, because Mr. Behan is a writer, not a talker. In speech, he is the man for the sharp rejoinder or the quick comment. He does recount some of his rejoinders, but he is modest and cannot go on telling you repeatedly how he did somebody else in the eye. As for the quick comment, it is exemplified by the typical and perfect caption to Mr. Hogarth's portrait of Mr. Behan as a Sad Thinker, which serves as frontispiece: "Brendan Behan after the lobster."

To return to the intervals: they consist of two short stories, which are childhood memories; an early play, "The Big House", which is not his best; two poems, and an Epilogue on the reactionary nature of the Church in Ireland.

The second story, "The Confirmation Suit", is a little work of art. It is presented as a true story, but Mr. Behan is obviously writing here instead of talking. The suit is a terrible one made for Brendan by Miss McCann, the shroud-maker, with almost no lapels and buttons "the size of saucers", and the climax is a telltale move by Brendan's mother who reports to Miss McCann that

Brendan is only pretending to wear this suit on weekends. She weeps. Later she dies, and young Brendan follows her coffin in the pouring rain, in the suit. "People said I would get my end, but I went on till we reached the graveside, and I stood in my Confirmation suit drenched to the skin. I thought this was the least I could do."

A final confession: many paragraphs in this book are devoted to attacking the "Anglo-Irish Horse-Protestants". I am one of these, if you take away the horse, and am therefore open to the accusation of exhibiting the prejudice and spite which have always been a feature of Irish literary life. But it does seem to me that "The Confirmation Suit" is art, and that the ballads, the Treaties, and the dimensions of the Phoenix Park and its all-the-year-round popularity are a waste of Mr. Behan's time and uncommon talent. And I don't care whether he calls it a "Sketchbook" or not. He also calls it *his* island—which is a bit hard on the horses.

*　　*　　*

iv. A Raucous, Witty Tour of Ireland by *Richard Ellmann**

Irish writers, if they happen to have been born poor, generally are middle class by the time they write travel books about Ireland. As a result, even when they think themselves critical, they often sound de-fanged.

Brendan Behan is not like those. He was born in the Dublin slums, "less than an ass' roar from Nelson's Pillar", he was a Borstal boy, he fought in the Irish Republican army, he was "on the run" for two years, he was imprisoned, and he is quite capable of taking part in another revolution.

The result is not an inveterate bitterness. Most of the time he is in fact laughing, and he confides that his ideal is to use palatable techniques of the music hall to convey by subterfuge something less palatable.

* *Chicago Sunday Tribune Magazine of Books*, (4 November 1962), p. 2

His book is full of ballads, poems, and jokes that exempt no group or degree; he seems to have forgotten none he ever has heard. When no ballad has been written to celebrate a hero or event, he writes one that more than serves. But in all the songs and stories he holds to the one idea, of looking at things from the bottom up.

Jonathan Swift may have been a pillar of eighteenth-century literature, but Behan celebrates him for his sympathy to the Dublin poor. He remembers Maud Gonne, who inspired Yeats' love poems, for mistreating his mother, who was her maid.

He knows Synge thru the Aran Islander who tried, unsuccessfully, to teach Irish to Synge. He is aware that De Valera once was a revolutionary like himself, but he cannot bear the "tweedy frugalities" to which he feels the Irish politician came at last.

The same attitude animates his descriptions of places to see. He evokes the Phoenix park not by naming its great official residences or fine prospects, but by remembering how the I.R.A. tried to blow up the statues of British generals there during the 'twenties and 'thirties.

That activity was "harmless enough," he remarks, and he compares the empty gesturing to the way the British once condemned him to death in his absence. "I sent them back a polite note saying they could shoot me in my absence also."

His truculent merriment culminates in a short play, "The Big House", which Behan interpolates in the middle of the book. He makes good, nasty fun in it of the Anglo-Irish, the English, and the Irish, too, especially the Irish who play along with the life of the big houses.

He offers no quarter to any of the characters and seems to share the delight of most of them in the ruin of the old order, no matter which way the spoils go.

A more difficult thing for Behan is to describe the Ireland he likes. This is a tough, witty, storytelling, singing, suffering, hard working Ireland, caught in his anecdotes and in Paul Hogarth's sketches.

If Behan [or the new Hogarth] has a danger, it is in liking these people too much. He is excellent in describing an old woman "bent in haggard prayer", but too tender when he notes "a pale, hunted look in her eyes". His prostitutes, gunmen, and clever, drinking men suit this humorous, savage talent best.

NOTE

1 The other autobiography reviewed is *West Briton*, by Brian Inglis.

9

Hold Your Hour and Have Another

i. Journalism by *Anon**

These short pieces written by Mr. Behan for the *Irish Press* in the mid-fifties have, as might be expected, far more vigour than most routine weekly journalism. The obsession with dialogue is given full rein; in particular the public-house conversation about war, revolution and poetry maintains a high euphoria—"I was through the lot, the Tan War, the Civil War, the Economic War", one character remarks—and the Joycean dislocations of language backfire hilariously at the great author of "Useless" himself. It was a happy idea to use Beatrice Behan's firm, expressive and admirably non-whimsical drawings with the text. Not only do they fit it well, making an uncommonly harmonious husband-and-wife production, but they are also well worth looking at in their own right.

* * *

ii. Wheezy Behan Humor by *Alan Pryce-Jones***

Once upon a time—some seventy years ago—there was a very successful book called "The Dolly Dialogues". In those days, the lower middle classes liked reading about the cultivated merriment of the rich. The late Anthony Hope thus did very well for himself by putting together a series of short newspaper pieces about the carryings-on of Dolly (Lady Mickleham), and her friends on and around Park Lane, London.

Nowadays, the upper classes are hypnotised by the earthier

* The *Times Literary Supplement* (London), (27 September 1963), p. 774.
** *New York Herald Tribune*, (28 January 1964), p. 19.

pleasures of the poor. And so a more modern newspaper, the Irish Press, commissioned from Brendan Behan a set of Dolly Dialogues in reverse. Instead of champagne, they breathe porter. Instead of driving in the brougham as far as Grosvenor Square, Mr. Behan's characters, when they are bold enough to leave the bar counter at all, stumble onto the bus for Dun Láoghaire. Mostly, however, they stand still and talk and sing after the manner of the late Victorian music-hall song: "Beg your parding, Mrs. Harding, Is my kitting In your garding?"

" 'He talks massive,' said Mrs. Brennan. 'You have to give him that.' " And we concede the point. Mr. Behan talks massive, all right, but like a lot of large men he is extremely light on his toes. He is, on the evidence, a natural writer, with a wonderful ear for idiom, a mind like a bee-hive, thrumming away nineteen to the dozen, and an engagingly generous spirit.

In his autobiography, "Borstal Boy", he showed how his qualities could be harnessed to build a minor masterpiece. These newspaper sketches, written in the middle 1950s, are no more than a preliminary canter. They are lazy at times. He has a favorite wry joke, "Carry on with the coffing, the corpse will walk," which turns up more than once, and some of the little sketches are worn to the thinness of words produced at the last moment against a deadline.

But, in a number of small touches, he builds up a living population of Dublin characters: Mrs. Brennan, Mr. Crippen and Maria Concepta the chief among them, all rattling on about nothing in particular with unquenchable verve. This is a Victorian art, going back to Dickens' Mr. Jingle, and Douglas Jerrold's Mrs. Caudle. To those who do not share the Dublin pub mystique it can be exasperating at times, and it includes a fair number of jokes which have already stood the test of time for a number of years.

But at his best Mr. Behan has a special kind of wheezy punning humor under taut control. He showed what he could do with it in the best parts of "The Hostage". Primarily he is a dialogue man, rather than a describer. "The Dolly Dialogues" are still amusing after all these years. It looks as though Mr. Behan's better fantasies will still carry a tickling flavor of sawdust and pipesmoke in the year 2030. They will be helped in this by Mrs. Behan's charming line drawings.

*   *   *

iii. The Side Streets of Dublin by *A. M. Sullivan**

There are two Brendan Behans in the lively bulk of the man from Dublin—the extrovert bumbler who worries friend and foe alike, and the shrewd observer of human nature in all its vagaries. Behan's observation is extremely alert to the auditory as well as the visual; his is a talent sensitive to the nuances of speech. While this skill was indicated in the bawdy text of *The Borstal Boy*, it is much more evident in *Hold Your Hour and Have Another*, where dialogue delineates character in the rowdy humor and ironic asides. Withal there is deep-seated compassion for fellow Irishmen, whether valid participants or pretentious frauds, in the "troubles" from 1916 to the end of the shooting. There are skilful bits of satire about the "other side", e.g., the muddled memory of Sammy Watt, who attended a Fenian meeting in Derry as a self-appointed spy intending to report on the treasonable opinions of "Dave O'Leary" —his own addled version of "De Valera".

This collection of sketches, which appeared in the Irish press between 1954 and 1956, constitutes brief excursions into minor turbulence. The swift eddies and shallows of the stream of humanity pass under an eye that finds some justification for every misfit, poseur, or knave. Behan's ear for the talk of Dublin pubs and tenements is as keen as John O'Hara's for the speech of middle-class urban dwellers in New York or Pennsylvania. One recognises the speech-flavor of O'Casey's *The Plough and the Stars* rather than that of Joyce's *Dubliners*, but Behan's skill in reporting the bizarre, the extravagant, and the maudlin is original, and gives a clue to his talent for stage dialogue.

Native Dubliners are competitive in conversation, and speak *ex cathedra* in the same sense as politicians, philosophers, and evangelists—they are always concerned with the possibility of being overheard by an appreciative audience. They praise, belittle, excoriate with a rare combination of metaphor and solecism. Behan captures much of this in his sketches, and not without affection for the men and women caught on the tines of his forked tongue. Mrs. Brennan, one of his favorites, says of her late husband: "In

* *Saturday Review* (New York), XLVII (8 February 1964), 39–40.

the British Milisha he was, my poor fellow, wasn't he, Maria Concepta? And a fine man, too."

"He was all that," said Maria Concepta, "and I heard my own fellow saying your fellow was as safe as houses in the war. He had only to put on his busby and march away. The Boers thought that it was a hedgehog moving."

The typical New Yorker may be at a loss in trying to follow the inferences, references, and innuendoes of Dublin idiom, although there are frequent notes identifying places and giving literal translations of Gaelic phrases. The language at times is almost as private as Limehouse Cockney; but the overtones and interlinear humor exude their flavor if not their full meaning.

If it were not for Behan's talent for transforming the trite, the absurd, and the nonsensical into rich farce, there would be no substance worth salvaging in many of these sketches; but his caricatures take on dimension and persist as characters long after one puts the book down. Here are people who mix wisdom and folly in a farrago that makes fascinating reading, once one is adjusted to the strange lingo.

10

The Scarperer

i. The Scarperer by *Richard Sullivan**

Ordinarily, a book review does not require a preface. But this one of Brendan Behan's only novel—if I understand his bibliography correctly—does, for four reasons.

First: An American writer bearing an Irish patronymic, reviewing a book by an Irish writer, may not be expected to praise all things Irish. If he did so he would be simply dishonest.

Second: Behan's reputation as a fine, generous, warm-hearted, roistering, hard-drinking lad seems to me to be higher currently than his reputation as a writer. He wrote, God rest him, very well. His writing must be praised. But I wonder whether he will be read a decade hence with anything like the acclaim he is getting now. I hold similar doubts about other writers whose lives seem to have outdone their committed words. Out of courtesy—for this is a preface to a review of a book by Brendan Behan—I name no other names.

Third: "The Scarperer", in an "afterword" signed by Rae Jeffs, is identified as a newspaper serial that ran for thirty days late last year in the *Irish Times*, under Behan's then-current pen name, Emmet Street. "Emmet Street"—so Behan is quoted in the afterword—"was the name opposite the street I was reared in, in North Dublin." This apparently is the first publication in book form of the novel, or crime story, which, the afterword suggests, gave Behan a little trouble in the writing.

Fourth: According to the publisher, by permission of Webster's Third New International Dictionary—which I summarise both in definitions and in etymologies listed—the noun "scarperer", as used for title, means something like a cunning man who arranges

* *Books Today (Chicago Tribune)*, (21 June 1964), p. 6.

168

escapes from prison over rugged walls, cliffs, and desperate slopes, for a pre-arranged price.

How Behan got hold of the old word is a mystery, quite as mysterious to an American reader as the slang and lingo used thruout the book. Surely, to one knowing, from the inside, the Dublin and the Paris of ten or so years back, this book holds a number of inside jokes. But for all practical purposes the "scarperer" is an Irish crook who manages the escape of an Englishman —the "Limey"—from an Irish prison.

Once the idiom is taken for granted, the story reads almost as well as one of Graham Greene's early "entertainments". As a story it goes along fast. In some spots it is funny. To its first Irish readers it must have been funnier than it is now to American readers, unable to catch all the local, temporal, and quickly passing references that comic writing usually makes. But it is loosely textured. It is not so much a plotted crime story as an ingenious farce upon all crime stories, past, present, and to come.

The Scarperer—I think—will not add much to Behan's standing as a writer. It is decently done hack work, by a man who had a gifted way with words even when, as here, he is writing about not much of anything except a prison escape and an interchange of identities between the escapee and a French gangster, along with a surprise ending involving "fifty-three million thousand" counterfeit French francs. There are some pleasant little touches, but there is nothing at all important or memorable or moving.

Yet it is good that this book has been made available. It casts some light in its way on the talent and the humor of a writer who had high vitality; and in its way it illuminates his better work, whether or not that work has, for the wrong reasons, been over-praised.

* * *

ii. Vintage Behan by *Jack White**

We Irish, they say, never appreciate our own: look at James Joyce, now, or Sean O'Casey. It may be true (I think it is) that

* The *Irish Times* (Dublin), (12 November 1966), p. 8.

jealousy is the national vice; but there is surely no evidence that we ever under-appreciated Brendan Behan. *The Quare Fellow* was first produced by Alan Simpson and Carolyn Swift at the Pike Theatre—though the published version claims the "first produc-tion" for the Theatre Royal, Stratford. *The Hostage* first appeared in Irish on the boards of the Damer. Behan's casual writings formed a lively column in the *Irish Press*, and this novel, *The Scarperer*, was written on commission for the *Irish Times*.

It was, in fact, commissioned by me. At that period—late 1953 —the *Irish Times* was making an effort to go "popular" by pub-lishing serial thrillers in daily instalments. The optimum run of a thriller seemed to be about five weeks, which meant thirty instal-ments or 30,000 words. As this is only about half the length of a normal novel, we found it more convenient to get our serials tailor-made at home. A good many were written by members of the staff, under various pseudonyms. I believe it was one of these versatile producers, Tony Gray, who suggested to me that I might commission a serial from Brendan Behan.

Brendan sent in a first chapter which was so funny that I made the deal at once: thirty instalments at three guineas each, ninety-odd pounds—to be paid, according to custom, on publication. Brendan, delirious at this vision of wealth, vanished to the Aran Islands, and chapters started coming in. Then (as Mrs. Rae Jeffs, Behan's Boswell, records in her introduction) his money ran out. He sent an S.O.S. to Westmorland street. "A few hours later," Mrs. Jeffs writes, "he collected ninety pounds from the post office. The *Irish Times* had not failed him and he was never to forget it."

After all those years, it is strange to see *The Scarperer* again— all in one piece this time, in hard covers and wearing a guinea ticket. In spite of this plutocratic dress, the story comes up just as it did at first—rich, robust, full of the scalding laughter of the Dublin streets. The ingenious plot begins with a planned escape (or scarper) from Mountjoy and moves on to Paris, where the climax is precipitated (a topical touch, this) by a benevolent lady interested in stopping the export of horses for slaughter. But the plot is only the bones of the thing: the joy lies in the comic zest of the story-teller. Behan sniffs at the aroma of the thieves' kitchen blissfully, like a kid smelling Bisto. It is rich in slang, in irony, in gallows humour.

The book is marked of course by its origins. It is short—thirty brief chapters, each with a cliffhang; it becomes a little aimless in the middle; and new characteres are introduced ex machina to achieve an ending. It has a Cast of Thousands; the straight ones, including the Scarperer himself, are dim enough, but the crazy ones are wonderful—Tralee Trembles, Pig's Eye O'Donnell, the Shaky Man, Glimmers Gleeson, Monsieur Tramtrack, the names themselves are a comedy. There is authentic Behan in Lugs, the thickest of the crooks, locked in his cell at last in Paris:

> "You're a frit pig," laughed Eddie Collins. "They'll have to carry you out if you're topped." "Everyone's frit of things like that," said Lugs. "I am frit by nature. I am the cowardliest man ever put foot in this cage and anything I ever done was only for the money."

This was Behan in his best period, before the exuberant talent had been sapped by booze. He gave good value for three guineas a thousand.

* * *

iii. Early and Late by *Desmond MacNamara**

In 1953 Brendan Behan was beginning to make a name as a writer of short stories and verse in English and Gaelic. He was also determined not to go back to housepainting and to this end he wrote an unusual thriller which was serialised by the *Irish Times*. He used the pseudonym of Emmet Street, but I never knew anyone who was fooled by that, and if there was, Brendan was well capable of correcting him.

He didn't like thrillers or know much about them, so he got round the difficulty by compounding a mixture of recollections, lags' lore and fantasy. Short of a character or a location, he would put down an account of his daily odyssey, squeezed, stretched and

* *New Statesman* (London), LXXII (18 November 1966), 750.

altered to make a further chapter. He was the kind of person who could make an epic out of buying a bus ticket. In *The Scarperer* I keep rediscovering afternoons and evenings in Dublin or Paris with a bit of story superimposed. Practically every character is recognisable in life, but the nearer they get to the central story the more he scrambled the data, perhaps to avoid libel, but more probably to avoid what he would describe as "a kick in the tacks". Twice, the Scarperer becomes himself, engaged in agreeable small talk with elderly ladies, an indulgence of his. The story is thin but he had a capacity for sketching in character and locale so that they dominate. Simenon does likewise.

11

Brendan Behan's New York

i. Hostage in New York by *Anon**

New York City has never yet been caught in a book. The most famous attempt was E. B. White's and for anyone who knows the depths of New York, his view is very much that of a middle-class commuter's. One handicap is that apart from bare-footed guide-books (and some of these scratch the surface most efficiently), only celebrities write about New York and a celebrity's world is too narrow, too self-centred. New York needs someone who has known it at most of its levels and in most of its colours, someone who has been willing to love and to suffer there as well as try to make his fortune: a Thomas Wolfe at the start of his career rather than at the end.

Brendan Behan was nearing the end of his bright celebrity's life when he came to do his book and the title itself is a pleasant confession of what we get: *Brendan Behan's New York*—or, considering his never-failing delight in the city, New York's Brendan Behan; anything but New York itself. The book, in fact, is like one of those extended chats with Mr. Behan in The Oasis on West 23rd Street, in which he wasted all the wit, gusto and feeling that one wished he had put into more literature. Yet those Oasis sessions should not be lost for people unlucky enough to miss them, and no tape-recorder could have caught them half so well as Mr. Behan does here.

"My neuroses are the nails and saucepans by which I get my living", he remarks, a tiny corner of the man suddenly being re-vealed behind the Irish blarney. It is not New York then he is brooding over but Mr. Behan, and it says much for Manhattan, if it ever needs such reflected glory, that it could draw him out more than anywhere else. The strain he felt at home in Dublin, the bitter-ness which his good humour kept under control in London, were

* The *Times Literary Supplement* (London), (22 October 1964), p. 955.

173

missing in Manhattan: even his drinking there had less of that hectic quality of a puritan suddenly let loose. "I had to plead that I had a hangover, which was a lie, because for a year in New York City I did not drink anything except soda water and tea." Perhaps no city on earth could have kept him so well entertained without more escapism, and in New York's effect on such a responsive visitor we learn something that is essential to New York: the city has a frightening habit of revealing itself only to the extent that you commit yourself. Mr. Behan never made any secret of his commitment, though he appreciated his handicap: he always remained a visiting celebrity there rather than an insider.

Some of the odd scraps of information he unloads as he rambles on are off-beat and useful, and they are delivered in a strangely reserved off-hand way, as if the Irish celebrity were really letting us in on a secret: that beneath Irish blarney lurked a person quite as reserved as the British. "I am told that not everyone all the time is happy, even in New York." That sounds more like Noël Coward than Brendan Behan. The note of detachment—of being "told" rather than directly experiencing—is unusual and perhaps ultimately explains Mr. Behan's difficulty in ever writing about New York. One has the same response to Mr. Hogarth's drawings which admirably match the text. They are neat and detailed and reflect a shrewd eye for the unusual angle on all these tourist scenes, but they are essentially the notes of a visitor, revealing in the end more of the artist than of the city. Brendan Behan's and Paul Hogarth's New York is no more and no less than the tributes of two visitors: the city still waits for the full confessions of an insider.

*　　*　　*

ii. Brendan Behan Gives Views of New York by *Robert Cromie**

Brendan Behan's New York [Bernard Geis, $5.95] is a rambling, garrulous sort of book which somehow I liked very much in spite of its failings. I don't know whether it is the thought of Brendan Behan roaming about Manhattan, watching things and drinking

* *Chicago Tribune*, (16 November 1964), Section 2, p. 2.

and having his own peculiar brand of fun, which pleases me, or whether it's the aura of good will which pervades the book, or whether it's that Behan wrote it—or perhaps dictated it—when he must have known he was not going to see New York, or anything else, very much longer.

Whatever the reason, the observing Behan eye and the pervasive Behan wit, plus the completely harmonious drawings of Paul Hogarth, blend into a book which should give you several pleasant hours of amusement and occasional instruction.

Behan tells, for example, what it's like to wait at Sardi's for the critical reports on opening night.

"Now if you get six out of six good reviews, you could ask the President of the United States to sell you the White House, tho I don't think this has ever happened. If you get five good reviews, you are doing fairly well and you have to start worrying about 480 Lexington av., which is the home of the income tax. It is not a bad kind of worry tho in its own way, if you have got to have worries, and I suppose everyone has to have them. If you have four, you can afford to give a party, or at least you can afford to attend the party which is usually given for you.

"If you get three good reviews, it's time to go home to bed, but if you get only two, you stay there the whole of the following day and don't go out until after dark. If you get one good review, you just make an air reservation very quickly to get back to where you came from, but if you get six bad reviews, you take a sleeping pill. You might even take an overdose."

Behan swims at the Y.M.C.A., visits Greenwich Village, pops in and out of numerous bars, chats with Jack Dempsey and Gene Tunney, James Thurber and Jack Kerouac, Arthur Miller, Nipsey Russell, Leonard Lyons, Black Muslems, Bowery bums, policemen, District Atty. Frank Hogan, Franchot Tone, and a great many other people of—to borrow an old and lovely phrase—high and low degree.

Parts of this long monolog about Manhattan and its inhabitants are, to give you fair warning, a little on the earthy side, but not over-balancingly so, and anyway, knowing Behan, this shouldn't surprise you.

175

One of my own favorite parts concerns McSorley's Old Ale House and Tim Costello's place, the latter fortunate enough to have some original Thurber drawings on its walls, a stout shillelagh [broken on purpose by Ernest Hemingway], and a hat once owned by the great John McNulty, a writer whose work will bear re-reading.

The book is a splendid tribute to New York, which Behan loved, and which he spoke of in this fashion:

> We don't come to a city to be alone, and the test of a city is the ease with which you can see and talk to other people. A city is a place where you are least likely to get a bite from a wild sheep and I'd say that New York is the friendliest city I know. The young Russian poet, Yevtushenko, said that in all honesty he had to admit that New York was the most exciting place that he had ever been to in his entire life.

The only time I ever saw Brendan Behan he was sound asleep in his publisher's office. I wish now I'd awakened him and said hello. He must have been fun. Troublesome, maybe, but fun.

12

Confessions of an Irish Rebel

i. Behan on Tape by *Maurice Richardson**

Only the soberest, most clear-headed writers are to be trusted with a tape-recorder. And even then the result may be woefully prolix. For the bibulous raconteur types this method of composition can prove fatal. This book was dictated by poor Behan towards the end of his days and edited after his death. Presumably it was intended as a supplement to his autobiography, *Borstal Boy*. It covers various periods of his life: in English and Irish prisons; doing odd jobs painting and decorating; hanging around in Paris; and acting as a deck hand on a boat that was supposed to be going to do some smuggling but rarely put to sea. It stops in 1955 just after his marriage and the production in Dublin of his play *The Quare Fellow*.

The writing, unfortunately, doesn't compare with that of *Borstal Boy*. There is a good deal of repetition and the continuity is jerky. There are plenty of stories but they give you the impression of having been half-remembered, half-invented. The prevailing effect is a bit laboured. It isn't, however, a depressing book to read. The personality of the genial Behan, which used in life to come at you in gusts of animal warmth like the steam from a Christmas pudding, manages to make itself felt.

*   *   *

ii. Confessions of an Irish Rebel by *Connolly Cole***

At first sight this book might give the impression that a good publisher was exploiting a good thing in printing Brendan Behan's

---

* The *Observer* (London), (7 November 1965), p. 27.
** *The Dublin Magazine*, V (Spring 1966), 95.

last tapes. But, reassuringly, it is veritable Behan—and, indeed, Behan, who was always a most spontaneous person, comes across very well in this sort of instantaneous autobiography. Mrs. Rae Jeffs' introduction is both friendly and understanding, and a debt is due her for the genuine labour she has put into this book.

Of course, in the strict sense, it is not an autobiography at all. I doubt if he could have written one, for Behan, like so many other good writers, was not sufficiently integrated a person for that. True, some account is given of his many brushes with law and authority, his internment at the Curragh, the shooting at Glasnevin, his early attempts at journalism and his emergence as a playwright during the days of the Pike Theatre, his marriage and, best of all, his several visits to France where, he once told me, he would like to live permanently. The French, the supreme individualists, must have regarded Brendan as one of their own.

As a sequel to *Borstal Boy*, perhaps his best and most sustained piece of writing, the present book flags. But it stands well on its own—and Dublin, and especially that side of Dublin which Behan knew as no one else, is described with amusement and affection, like a Bangkok of the West, highly impractical, wholly charming and slightly mad.

This is unlikely to be the last posthumous Behan book, and if they are all as good as this his reputation as one of our best and most humorous writers will remain secure. There is no question about it: this is real Behan—his gusto, gaiety, compassion and even innocence are still here, palpable and infectious. And so is his extraordinary talent, still vigorous, roistering and full—and still needing slightly to be rinsed.

*   *   *

iii. Brendan Behan by *Stanley Weintraub**

In a pre-electronic age, this sequel to *Borstal Boy* is one of those memoirs which would have been fated to remain unwritten. Someone had once warned Behan, "You'll kill yourself more with drink

* *Books Abroad*, XLI (1967), 227–228.

than with the I.R.A."; and to a London publisher who had Behan's signature on a contract the prophecy looked too true to be good. A transistorised rescue operation seemed the solution, and a determined lady was dispatched to tape the increasingly besodden garrulities of Ireland's answer to Dylan Thomas. The printed result is a triumph of a sort. Except for a few uncharacteristic lines, *Confessions of an Irish Rebel* is Behan at his most flavoursome—like listening in on a well-oiled Brendan singing and talking and chortling his autobiographical way through a merry evening in a Dublin pub.

Rae Jeffs, the book's editor, offers the prefatory explanation that *Confessions* "was recorded on tape . . . and was transcribed and edited after his death. It may, consequently, lack the final polish Brendan would have wished. But it is all his. . . ." Nevertheless, a report from London quotes the editor as confessing that the memoir was prepared "with the aid of additional material which he wrote at different times and anecdotes which he told me and which I have reproduced as much as possible in his own words." This probably accounts for the narrative's being filled out with what amounts to a remarkable anthology of vintage Behan stories and songs, political and historical, bibulous and blasphemous. Brendan would have liked the general effect.

13

Richard's Cork Leg

i. Behan Play with Hardly a Leg to Stand On by *J. J. Finegan**

The play that Godot-like, became a Dublin legend for non-appearance, *Richard's Cork Leg*, has finally reached the stage at the Peacock.

It is, of course, Brendan Behan's last theatrical excursion. He completed one act; the other was stitched together by Alan Simpson from notes and sketches found some time ago.

CONGLOMERATION

It was quickly apparent that for all its similarity with the pattern and style of *The Hostage* (was Brendan trying to repeat the world-wide success of that work?) this posthumous conglomeration bears little comparison with that earlier, exhilarating piece.

Richard's Cork Leg is Brendan with his inspiration ebbing fast, and precariously. Were it not for the songs, up to twenty of them, it would be a very thin evening indeed.

Of plot there is hardly a vestige. A couple of Dublin prostitutes visiting a cemetery met up with a collection as bizarre as themselves—two supposedly blind men, some Blueshirts from the 1930s, a red-shirted fighter from the Spanish Civil War, and a highly-suspect member of an obscure sect to whose Union Jack-festooned home they all congregate for drinks and a long sing-song.

The Dubliners are the backbone of the romp—I hesitate to term it a play. As musicians the famous five are, need it be said, in their own inimitable class. As actors, however, the competition from the Abbey actresses who surround them is pretty severe.

The cast includes Eileen Coogan, Joan O'Hara, Angela Newman,

* *Evening Herald* (Dublin), (15 March 1972), p. 4. This is a review of the world premiere at the Peacock Theatre, Dublin, 14 March 1972, during the Dublin International Theatre Festival.

Derbhla Molloy and Terri Donnelly and design by Wendy Shea, with lighting by Leslie Scott.

* * *

ii. A Behan Celebration by *Robert Brustein**

Richard's Cork Leg was begun by Brendan Behan in 1961, and left unfinished at his death in 1964. Now reconstructed and completed by Alan Simpson, the director of the Abbey Theatre's production at the Royal Court, it seems almost old-fashioned in its irrepressible animal spirits. Behan's gifts as a dramatist were no more orderly than his life as a drunkard. What emerges most vividly from his plays is the jocular-querulous, clamorous-melodious atmosphere of a Dublin pub. *Richard's Cork Leg* has all the theatrical significance of a pint of ale—sometimes full of yeasty ferment, sometimes merely full of boozy conviviality. An amiable shambles, the evening is nevertheless brimming with pleasure, overflowing with goodnatured, bubbling zip.

It is typical of the shiftlessness of the work that its eponymous hero never appears. He is, in fact, mentioned only once in passing when one of the characters, a whore named Rose of Lima, tells of a former husband whose leg was shot off by the British. When they first went to bed together, Rose felt the cork replacement, and not knowing what it was, said dauntlessly, "Give us a glass of water and I'll chance it." This tone of goofy incontinence is matched only by the play's extravagant characters and setting. Located primarily in a Dublin cemetery, it is populated with Behan's familiar personae of loquacious prostitutes, nubile maidens, puritanical Protestants, phoney blind men, Irish revolutionaries and fascists, and a black mortician, on loan from California's Forest Lawn, who specialises in singing corpses.

As usual, the author compensates for his lack of plot by substituting rhetoric and wit, comic seductions, drunken parties, hoary jokes, and a large number of songs, most of them written by Behan

* The *Observer* (London), (24 September 1972), p. 36.

181

to a variety of folk and classical tunes, and performed by a quintet called the Dubliners on a variety of stringed instruments.

The only organising principle in this gallimaufry is the presence of death, which still retains its customary sting-aling-aling—sex and death (seductions occur on top of gravestones); wealth and death (one corpse is "poxy with money", but as Rose says, "he can kiss my royal Irish arse for all the good his money will do for him now"); science and death ("Go easy with your experiments", cautions a corpse, "or you'll be seeing me sooner than you expect"); and, above all, death and revolutionary politics. For Behan, who saw a bit of such action himself, "graveyards and patriots always go together", and, very frequently, the innocent get pushed below the turf as well. In the climax of the play, one character mistakenly receives a fusillade intended for a revolutionary; and although he pops up immediately (in typical Behan fashion) for a post-mortem finale, his future singing career, as well as his capacity to drink and fornicate, have been sadly terminated.

The production is quite brilliant, directed with headlong energy and impeccably acted, especially by Joan O'Hara and Eileen Coogan as the two whores, and by Luke Kelly and Ronnie Drew as the two ersatz blind men (Drew sings six of the songs, snapping a hoarse bass-baritone at the tunes like a bull-whip). A fine memorial to its dead author's love of life, *Richard's Cork Leg* is also an almost anachronistic celebration of unconditioned man—mortal, fallible, self-preserving, yet vivid in his whiskey-soaked humanity.

*　　*　　*

iii. Death and the Irish by *Anon**

Brendan Behan's posthumous *Richard's Cork Leg* is concerned with Irish patriotism and political violence. Despite its idiosyncratic and rambling form, far looser than the more fully realised *The Hostage*, this remains a play of the 1960s, unfinished and somewhat arbitrarily assembled from the fragments Behan left at his death ten years ago. Curiously, it is a more innocent work

* The *Times Literary Supplement* (London), (26 April 1974), p. 441. This is a review of the published version of the play.

than *The Hostage*, with satirical jabs which seem mild in the light of the day's headlines, while the earlier work is as timely as ever.

Behan's work is about living in the midst of death. In *Richard's Cork Leg*, most of the action takes place in a Dublin graveyard, which becomes a Gaelic pantheon populated by a Black American mortician, whores, the chronically unemployed and patriots. Plot is almost an accidental factor, though there are two shootings, a seduction and a confrontation between Blueshirt supporters of Franco and a lone Irish supporter of the Spanish Republic. What matters is the telling and here the play is splendid Behan, ribald and stuffed full of old jokes, new songs, bad puns and contagious irreverence.

Behan slings barbs in all directions: "Casement? You know that he was a homosexual was proved by the British Government. . . . The Committee were all old Etonians who knew about it." Or: "Other people have a nationality. The Irish and Jews have a psychosis." Or the "blessed Evelyn Waugh. She was a young girl that wouldn't marry Henry the Eighth because he turned Protestant." While Behan's attitude toward political violence is finely summed up by a "Bawd" who thinks "graveyards and patriots go together".

Alan Simpson of the Abbey Theatre in Dublin assembled the several versions of the play into this published edition, and on the whole he has done it well, though at times in his introduction he seems a bit prouder of his own surgery than of Behan's original text. Nor is the surgery impeccable. Behan, for example, never wrote an ending, though he left a note suggesting that the chief character, Cronin, would die. Mr. Simpson has chosen to end the play with this death, but it is merely a casual piece of violence, an accidental shooting made comic by Mr. Simpson's addition of ominous faces at the window and blundering meter-readers, while the ending Behan himself had prepared through the earlier action was potentially more poignant and truly comic.

Index